POWER FOR TODAY (VOL. 1)
Practical Spirituality For Everyday Living

Dr. Lee Ann B. Marino, Ph.D., D.Min., D.D.

Published by:
Righteous Pen Publications
The righteousness of God shall guide my pen
www.righteouspenpublications.com

All rights reserved. Except as permitted under the U.S. Copyright Act of 1976, no part of this book may be reproduced, distributed, or transmitted in any form or by any means, electronic or mechanical, or saved in any information storage and retrieval system without written permission from the author.

Unless otherwise noted, Scriptures taken from the **Holy Bible, New International Version ®, NIV® (1984),** Copyright © 1973, 1978, 1984, 2011 by Biblica, Inc.™ Used by permission of Zondervan. All rights reserved worldwide.

All passages marked KJV are taken from the **Holy Bible, Authorized King James Version,** Public Domain.

All passages marked AMPC are taken from **The Amplified® Bible (AMPC),** Copyright © 1954, 1958, 1962, 1964, 1965, 1987 by The Lockman Foundation. Used by permission. (www.Lockman.org)

All passages marked ESV are taken from the **Holy Bible, English Standard Version®,** Copyright © 2001 by Crossway, a publishing ministry of Good News Publishers. All rights reserved. Used by permission.

All passages marked ASV are from the **American Standard Version of the Holy Bible,** 1901. Public domain.

All passages marked CEB are taken from the **Common English Bible®, CEB®** Copyright © 2010, 2011 by Common English Bible. ™ Used by permission. All rights reserved worldwide. The "CEB" and "Common English Bible" trademarks are registered in the United States Patent and Trademark Office by Common English Bible. Use of either trademark requires the permission of Common English Bible.

All passages marked NASB are taken from **The New American Standard Bible®,** Copyright © 1960, 1962, 1963, 1968, 1971, 1972, 1973, 1975, 1977, 1995 by The Lockman Foundation. Used by permission.

All passages marked GW are a copyrighted work of **God's Word to the Nations.** Quotations are used by permission. Copyright 1995 by God's Word to the Nations. All rights reserved.

Book Classification: Books > Religion & Spirituality > Christian Books & Bibles > Christian Living > Inspirational

Copyright © 2016, 2025 by Dr. Lee Ann B. Marino.

ISBN: 1-940197-43-0
13-Digit: 978-1-940197-43-2

Printed in the United States of America. All rights reserved.

Dedication

I dedicate this first volume of my Power For Today anthology to every writer who has ever written for our magazine — every reader — every believer who has come away from this work with joy and a deeper walk with the Lord — and every person who has read and has walked away from this magazine, knowing there is a God that they must believe in to walk in power and experience true freedom.

So here is to all of us involved in Power For Today Magazine — past, present, and future — writers, readers, distributors, editors, staff of all sorts, fans from season to season, and friends both old, new, and yet to come.

TABLE OF CONTENTS

	Introduction...	1
1	The Lord Is My Shepherd...But Still Do I Want (December 2011).	3
2	When Jesus Returns (December 2010).................................	11
3	Wisdom Cries Out (January 2010).......................................	19
4	Paradigm Shift (January/February 2013)..............................	27
5	Lord, Teach Me To Pray! (August 2010)...............................	35
6	The Power Of Suggestion (May/June 2014)..........................	43
7	The Center Of His Will (First Quarter 2015).........................	51
8	Discerning Discernment (October 2011)..............................	59
9	Class Action (January 2011)..	67
10	Discerning Wise And Foolish Behavior (July/August 2012)......	75
11	Searching For The Immortal In All The Mortal Places (January 2007)..	83
12	Confident Of Better Things (November 2011).......................	89
13	Representing Christ (May/June 2013)..................................	97
14	Moving Up Higher! (October 2009).....................................	105
15	Enjoying Your Spouse (July/August 2013)............................	113
16	My Own Way Never Really Mattered Anyway! (May/June 2012)....	121
17	Holiness (January/February 2014)......................................	129
18	Holding Onto Hope In The Midst Of Hopelessness (March 2010)	137
19	The Seven Churches Of Revelation, Part 1 (Third Quarter 2015)..	145
20	The Seven Churches Of Revelation, Part 2 (Fourth Quarter 2015)	153

21	Unity (June 2010)..	161
22	Praise God ANYWAY! (April 2009)......................................	169
23	Hospitality (July 2011)...	177
24	The Battle Belongs To The Lord (July 2010)..........................	185
25	It's The End Of The World As We Know It (Fourth Quarter 2014)..	193
	About The Author: Dr. Lee Ann B. Marino, Ph.D., D.Min., D.D...	203

INTRODUCTION

Power For Today Magazine started out as the *Power For Today* Newsletter in April of 2002. Its original purpose was to update people monthly who knew about Apostle (then Pastor, although often using the title of Evangelist) Marino's work. Our initial mail run was around one hundred copies, all written, edited, laid out, copied, stuffed, and mailed to everyone who was on our mailing list at the time. Most of that work was completed by Apostle Marino herself, as the newsletter's content hadn't been open to freelance writers yet. The mailing list consisted mostly of family, friends, and people that Apostle had met along the way in her research for religion and a few people here and there who had expressed interest in her work as an independent minister. The first edition had the theme of change, and her cover article was titled, *Many Are Called, But Few Get Up*. As it challenged conventional ideas about church and religious involvement, its reception was mixed. Some liked it, some disliked it; and there were those who went on to absolutely reject it, in every form.

Regardless of the mixed response, the work continued to grow. *Power For Today* plowed on as a monthly magazine, featuring insights, teaching, and devotional thoughts for individuals of varying denominations. Topics such as the end times, the nation of Israel, prayer, obedience to God, control, and commitment to the work of God might not seem like very controversial topics, but in the early 2000s, such topics were not common for discussion. Whether people loved it or hated it, the work sparked interest and intrigue and caused thought and inspiration among those who read its contents.

Our work shifted from a six-page newsletter to one that was eight pages, and within about three years, went from being a newsletter to a magazine. The work of the magazine developed through those years, becoming longer and improved through designs and formats. As the magazine changed and developed, the initial mailing list changed many times over, growing, shrinking, growing and shrinking again, all up until the advances of the internet made it possible for *Power For Today* Magazine to reach many more people than ever imagined. Since our start online, *Power For Today* Magazine has been seen in over seventy countries worldwide through both print and electronic distribution. We also opened up the magazine's contents to outside writers, allowing for guest columns, articles, and thoughts to inspire and encourage those who read its pages.

In October 2010, *Power For Today* Magazine celebrated its one hundredth issue with a special retrospect look-back over the history of the magazine and its influence as a literary powerhouse. There were points in the early history of the magazine when it wasn't believed it would turn into anything viable, so reaching one hundred issues was a monumental breakthrough in the history of the work and the history of the ministry. In July 2014, *Power For Today* Magazine merged with *Women of Power* Magazine and *Apocalypse Watch* Journal, forming one magazine, published four times per year. Over the two years between our magazine merger and the cessation of publication, *Power For Today's* content has continued to bless readers, delight audiences, and provide voice and insight to both new and seasoned writers.

Today, *Power For Today* Magazine is a true showcasing of the diversity and beauty present within the work of Apostolic Fellowship International Ministries. Complete with interviews, regular articles and columns from those covered by the ministry, guest writers and interviews, and many different devotional and inspirational sections, *Power For Today* Magazine continued, through sixteen years of publication. Even though publication has now ceased, it is still used for Bible studies, as a teaching tool, a reference guide, and to keep up with the revelatory words that come forth from those who contribute to this work.

Thus, we are pleased to present this first-volume of our Editor-in-Chief's articles from *Power For Today* Magazine. Spanning over ten years of revelation, insight, and growth, this work reflects not just her writing as an author, but her development as a minister. Going through as we grow in God is never easy, and the cover articles written by Apostle Marino herself document and reveal that journey to both spiritual and ministerial discovery. Through the thoughts, the rejections, the difficulties and the trials, we see the end result of it all: the making of a minister with a ministry that now impacts lives throughout the United States and all over the world.

(The Editors of *Power For Today* Magazine)

Moreover [let us also be full of joy now!] let us exult and triumph in our troubles and rejoice in our sufferings, knowing that pressure and affliction and hardship produce patient and unswerving endurance. And endurance (fortitude) develops maturity of character (approved faith and tried integrity). And character [of this sort] produces [the habit of] joyful and confident hope of eternal salvation. Such hope never disappoints or deludes or shames us, for God's love has been poured out in our hearts through the Holy Spirit Who has been given to us.
- Romans 5:3-5 (AMPC)

THE LORD IS MY SHEPHERD...
BUT STILL DO I WANT
(Volume 10, No. 12 – December 2011)

If anyone hangs around on the internet, they will encounter the phenomenon of the "right" Christian. If you've encountered this type, you know exactly who I am talking about. You would think these individuals believe Christianity lies in being right, rather than being saved. Everything turns into an argument - and big, major arguments, at that. Nothing is simple, and all roads lead right back to whatever their opinion may be about whatever topic it is that may be at hand. You can't disagree with them about anything - not politics, not social issues, not anything - or they think you're not going to heaven. They deal in pride, arguments, anger, frustration, and are a giant headache for everyone else.

A few years ago, I was on an international prayer website that posted people's prayer requests online for the worldwide Christian community could raise up the petitions. Don't get me wrong - I think this is a nice enough idea. In the right hands, it can pull people out of the isolation they find in their little, immediate communities and draw people into something bigger and deeper than themselves. The only problem was that the site was clearly not monitored for content, as some of the petitions were extremely ridiculous. One of these ridiculous petitions stood out: "Pray that God removes my $50,000 worth of debt and makes me debt free." My first thought was, "Hey! God didn't get you into that - you are not going to tell me God told you to go and get yourself $50,000 in debt. Why should it be His job to get you out?!"

Even though it's been a few years since I saw that petition, it was not the last time I encountered a "debt Christian." I meet many ministers, believers, churchgoers, and those who are somewhere in-between who have amassed thousands of dollars' worth of debt because they felt like they should have "stuff." Then they rack up severe financial consequences, only seek the ability to "pray" the debt away.

Everywhere I turn I see Christians fighting over who is right about matters that don't matter, ministers who claim to be about ministry, yet have never seen the outside of a pulpit, and a general spirit of nastiness, unpolished poise, unhappiness, stress, strife, and anger. What is behind these cycles of control - whether it's to be right, ignore consequences, or amass things?

Unsatisfied

It seems that I meet people daily who are "believing God" for things: a new car, a new house, a new dress, a better job, a pay raise, a relationship of one sort or another, fame, ministry promotion, and most of all, the combination of all the above: fortune. Christians today seem preoccupied with "things." The non-Christian world often brands modern Christians as selfish, greedy individuals who only use their faith to get things, not to make a difference in this world. Christians who "exercise faith" for things believe they are just doing what they are allowed to do as believers. Who is right here? Are Christians entitled to have whatever they want? Is the secular world right about its current impression of Christianity? Or is something more at play here?

No matter what side of the debate you may fall on, one thing is definite: Christians aren't satisfied with Jesus, they aren't satisfied in their relationship with God, and they aren't satisfied to have their needs met. They want to be right, they want everyone to

> ### BEHIND THE ARTICLE
>
> It has always been deeply important to me that we develop a deep, abiding understanding of the spiritual things of God. When it came time to write an article for the Christmas edition in 2011, the only thing I could think about was the materialism I saw and the way that materialism has crept into the believer's life on a regular basis. Even though materialism is a common theme for Christmas discussion, it is something that hits the lives of believers on a regular basis. If we want to be truly changed people, then we need to allow God to work within us so we can overcome our need for things and grow in faith.

know and agree that they are right, they want an abundance of things, and they even want a mythical Santa Claus to come and make everything all right, at least once per year.

The Israelites in Haggai's time were too a discontented and dissatisfied people. They lived in captivity for many years and spent numerous years attending to themselves upon returning to Israel. To the Israelites in this time frame, it was all about building houses for themselves and filling those houses with many things to fill their lives. In their wild pursuit of things, they totally forgot about God. The Prophet Haggai rose up in this time to call God's people back to Him, echoing words worth hearing in this age as well: *Give careful thought to your ways. You have planted much, but have harvested little. You eat, but never have enough. You drink, but never have your fill. You put on clothes, but are not warm. You earn wages, only to put them in a purse with holes in it. This is what the LORD Almighty says: 'Give careful thought to your ways. Go up into the mountains and bring down timber and build the house, so that I may take pleasure in it and be honored,' says the LORD. 'You expected much, but see, it turned out to be little. What you brought home, I blew away. Why?' declares the LORD Almighty. 'Because of my house, which remains a ruin, while each of you is busy with his own house. Therefore, because of you the heavens have withheld their dew and the earth its crops. I called for a drought on the fields and the mountains, on the grain, the new wine, the oil and whatever the ground produces, on men and cattle, and on the labor of your hands.* (Haggai 1:5-11)

The endless pursuit of more, more, more has its consequences. We forget to seek God and ignore His Kingdom. When we insist on being headstrong and selfish, it always reaches a point where God intervenes in their endless want by speaking to them through lack.

The First Church of More

We're seeing a phenomenon today unparalleled to any other time in history: the preacher or minister who taps into genuine human want rather than genuine human need. The result of such a tap is a church very, very in touch with what they want, but very, very out of touch with what they need physically, spiritually, and emotionally - and a severe departure from

---

KEY VERSE: GALATIANS 2:20

I am crucified with Christ: nevertheless I live; yet not I, but Christ liveth in me: and the life which I now live in the flesh I live by the faith of the Son of God, Who loved me, and gave Himself for me. (KJV)

doctrine and teaching. The blurring of such causes Christians to expect God to live as a "Santa Claus" type figure, ready at any time to give them exactly what they want on demand. 2 Timothy 4:3-4 warns of such a time: *For the time will come when men will not put up with sound doctrine. Instead, to suit their own desires, they will gather around them a great number of teachers to say what their itching ears want to hear. They will turn their ears away from the truth and turn aside to myths.* Very seldom do we hear any doctrine or teaching today - in particular, we seldom hear much about walking the Christian life or about living by Christian principle - instead, we hear about how to get more "stuff" from God and what we "deserve" as believers. God is our Father, Jesus is our Savior, we are redeemed and on our way to heaven, and yet people want more...and more. The Lord is their Shepherd, but still do they want. It's not uncommon to see individuals transfer their pre-salvation wants and desires over to God, expecting Him to make all their wants - past, present, and future - materialize.

Such severe dissatisfaction among so-called believers is a sign of a greater problem than may appear on the surface. Christians today are experiencing greed that, while not a new phenomenon, is justified by teachers of faith today. Rather than dispelling greed, greed is encouraged as a spiritual pursuit. Disguised as the new prosperity, greed is becoming the spiritual passion of those unwilling to take the next step toward spiritual things. Who would dispel such an argument? Anyone truly versed in the Scriptures: *But you, keep your head in all situations, endure hardship, do the work of an evangelist, discharge all the duties of your ministry.* (2 Timothy 4:5) It is time, once and for all, for Christians to discover the principle of "not want."

True prosperity is not discovering want after want after want and seeking all of those wants to be met. If we read and properly understand the Scriptures pertaining to prosperity, they speak of a lack of want - not an increase in it. The proper precept is that God is with us and we abide by His principles, thus He meets our needs and wants in our lives. True prosperity is the ability to sit back and realize not that we have yet another want, but that we have no wants as all we need, God has already given to us.

We trust God for the things we don't have and thank Him for the things we do have. The message to us today? We need to be less enamored with things and more enamored with God. Maybe we need to have less of other things for awhile and have more of just Jesus!

I have been crucified with Christ

Galatians 2:20 gives Christians a sobering word on the Christian life: *I am crucified with Christ: nevertheless I live; yet not I, but Christ liveth in me: and the life which I now live in the flesh I live by the faith of the Son of God, Who loved me, and gave Himself for me.* (KJV) The Christian life is not one where we can simply live as we used to, pursuing the same intense wants. The Apostle Paul's point of being crucified with Christ indicates the Christian to die to the flesh, and now live with Christ inside. It is a shift in pursuit, shifting from chasing after wants to now chasing after the things which glorify God and Christ. Such as death in self to Christ unites us to Him and with His intentions and pursuits. Having such an experience turns one's life around and also changes one's perspective on what is important in life. True Christians don't chase and pursue the world, and they certainly don't disguise such pursuits as holy, faith-filled endeavors. Christians are called to call greed just what it is - greed - and amend such tendencies and behaviors, while relying on the life we have in Christ to lead us into all truth.

Being crucified with Christ doesn't mean that we stop having normal needs. It doesn't mean that we will never want another thing again as long as we live. It also doesn't mean that it's good to ignore genuine needs that we, as people or even ministers, may have. What it does mean is that we trust God for what we need, rather than relying on earthly means to get it. It also means that we stop measuring ourselves against worldly standards. It's unrealistic to suppose that everyone is called to live like a hip-hop artist or music mogul. We learn through the parable of the talents that not everyone can handle the same number of resources as someone else, and as we stand crucified with Him, we come to a place of contentment. Some things aren't needed right now. Some things aren't for this time or place. Some things aren't needed, period. We place ourselves and our priorities in the Father's hands, trusting that whatever is needed will be met.

You can't always get what you want....so seek first the Kingdom!

Over forty years ago, the Rolling Stones sang about a very poignant aspect of reality: you can't always get what you want. This fact of life doesn't change when we become Christian; Christian or not, we don't always get what we think we want or even what we think we need in life. What does change when we experience a genuine conversion turn-around is our understanding of want and need. Knowing God in a personal way (personal as in for ourselves) and knowing Jesus both change our outlook on life. While we may not always get what we want, we understand better why we may not get what we want. We see the lessons God delivers to us through our experiences. Most importantly, we can rest in the assurance of knowing God will provide what we need and be satisfied with what we have rather than always seeking something more. Seeing Matthew 6:33-34 as a stern halting to greed certainly puts excessive want in perspective: *But seek first the Kingdom of God, and His righteousness; and all these things shall be added unto you. Take therefore no thought for the morrow: for the morrow shall take thought for the things of itself. Sufficient unto the day is the evil thereof.* (KJV) There is plenty for us to consider, preoccupy ourselves with, and dwell upon for today; we do not need to be worried about what we don't have or what we should want. Focusing on God's Kingdom and living that everyday takes the focus off what you may want and places it squarely where our focus should reside: on Christ.

God doesn't buy us

> **AUTHOR'S REFLECTIONS**
>
> The Twenty-Third Psalm of the Bible is commonly invoked at funerals to inspire comfort and hope for those who have had a departed loved one. We forget, however, that it is also here to comfort and encourage the living. If we trust God's assurances for our salvation, then surely we should trust them for our lives.

The bottom line of all of this? Just like we can't buy our salvation, God doesn't buy us, either. God is not a doting grandfather, father, or boyfriend. The Christian life isn't a big bartering system by which we are immediately rewarded with things for having faith. Greed is still a sin because it is the pursuit of things above and beyond God and what He wants for us in our lives. So much in this world is bought or exchanged with money, but God isn't one of those things. What's more, so much of what really matters in this life isn't bought or sold. The proof of this can be seen in the multitude of lives spent in misery despite millions of dollars. It is only when we see that life is more than money and things that we can truly reach the point where we see beyond our own wants. There is so much need in this world and we can't begin to reach out and meet some of those needs until we get our minds off our own needs and wants all the time. Trusting God for no more in life than things minimizes the whole of the work He is doing within us and through us as we reach out to others. In a world where more than three quarters of its people live below the poverty level, the last thing we need is a greedy, self-centered, uncharitable church. God wants to see Christians elevate to a level where they are not bribed by money, not swayed by cars or fancy clothes, and not intimidated by the giants of this world who throw their weight around with money. Becoming that kind of a person means we get past the televangelist mentality that money is the only way God reaches out to us and meets our needs here on earth. God is good all the time - when we have lack, when we have more than enough, and for every other condition we will encounter in between.

The Lord is my Shepherd, I shall not want

Realizing that God is our Shepherd is quite a realization. Shepherds care for and tend to sheep, whether they deserve it or not, no matter how stubborn they may be, or how difficult they may be to deal with. We can all look back and realize how far we've come and how much God has worked in us only when we stop measuring ourselves by how much stuff we have. Surely, God does provide, and we should acknowledge Him for that; but God also does so much that we can't measure by a monetary currency or by how much money we may have in the bank.

    I pray that we shall all reach the point where we realize if God never did another thing for us in our lives, He's done enough in sending His Son, Jesus, to be the atonement for our sins. Maybe rather than making Christmas wish lists and hurriedly shopping at this time of year, we should sit back and think about the work God has done for us. It is only in this realization that we can truly say, *The LORD is my Shepherd; I shall not want. He maketh me to lie down in green pastures: He leadeth me beside the still waters. He restoreth my soul: He leadeth me in the paths of righteousness for His Name's sake. Yea, though I walk through the valley of the shadow of death, I will fear no evil: for Thou art with me; Thy rod and Thy staff, they comfort me. Thou preparest a table before me in the presence of mine enemies; Thou anointest my head with oil; my cup runneth over. Surely goodness and mercy shall follow me all the days of my life: and I will dwell in the house of the LORD forever.* (Psalm 23:1-6, KJV)

Apostle Marino ministering in Daytona Beach, Florida (August 2014)

WHEN JESUS RETURNS
(Volume 9, No. 12 – December 2010)

*I*n the movie *Talladega Nights: The Ballad Of Ricky Bobby*, Ricky Bobby's character prays a particularly memorable grace prior to eating a holiday meal. Multiple times he addresses the prayer to "Dear Lord baby Jesus," "Dear little baby Jesus," "baby Jesus powers," "tiny infant Jesus," "Christmas Jesus," "dear tiny Jesus in your golden fleece diapers and your tiny little balled-up fist," "dear eight-pound, six-ounce newborn infant Jesus, don't even know a word yet, just little infant so cuddly, but still omnipotent," and "dear baby God." When his wife pointed out to him that Jesus was no longer a baby and it was rather odd to keep praying to a baby, he defensively responded with, "I like the Christmas Jesus best, and I'm saying grace. When you say grace, you can say it to grown-up Jesus, or teenage Jesus, or bearded Jesus, or whoever you want." When his wife's father confronted him about Jesus being a man, Ricky Bobby says, "I like the Christmas version the best, DO YOU HEAR ME?!" This spun off into other various images people at the table had of Jesus, including seeing Jesus in a tuxedo T-shirt which says "formal, but I like to party," and his son saying he likes to picture Jesus as a ninja, fighting off evil samurai! As if this wasn't bad enough, one at the table said they like to picture Jesus with huge golden wings, singing lead for Lynrd Skynrd, like an angel band!

Most people see a spectacle such as this and laugh at the various innuendos present. Others see it as a total blasphemy and disregard for the power of prayer and the ability to call on the Name of the Lord. No matter how any one of us may feel about the holidays, prayer, or theology, we can see serious theological flaws in the dinner prayer in *Talladega Nights*. The character's responses to Jesus resound a total distortion of Jesus in His personage and ministry. No matter how many years pass, how many other images will come along of Christ, or how many he's seen, "Christmas Jesus" will forever be his favorite, the eternal image of a baby in a manger rather than a returning King.

Many echo similar thoughts about Jesus. The idea of embracing Jesus as a baby rather than a grown Savior is more appealing because we idolize the newness of life present in babies. They enjoy the idea of Jesus as formidable and controllable as an infant. The idea of Jesus returning as a King, in power and great glory, coming as a judge and ruler, does not appeal to those who do not desire to confront themselves or their lack of obedience. As a result, they have created doctrines to conform to their comforts.

There is clear confusion in the world about Jesus' return and His nature now. Many believe Jesus is returning as a baby, to start life over again, in a sort of reincarnation sense. They see the Christmas holiday not just as an advance of the first advent, but the second as well. Others believe Jesus is returning to usher in a "new age" where all religions come to recognize commonalities and all other religious leaders shall also return and usher in an age of "enlightenment." Some believe Jesus is coming back to redeem them exclusively, damning the rest of existence to hell or a state of non-existence. Still others believe Jesus' return is nonexistent, a mere figment of clever imagery, and He will never come back and therefore it's irrelevant how He shall return or what He will do once He is here.

Our image of Jesus is very important, especially as we recognize He is coming again very soon. We need to know Who we are looking for, and how He shall come in His return. How do you regard Jesus? When you pray to Him, do you see a baby in a manger, or a powerful, soon-returning Savior? Every year people remember Jesus as a baby in a manger...but

> **BEHIND THE ARTICLE**
>
> I was struggling with an idea for the December 2010 issue, as I wanted to deviate from our standard Christmas-themed issue for the first time in our history. Because talk of Christmas often inspires thoughts about the Second Coming, a recall from the dinner prayer in the movie *Talladega Nights* inspired an entire thought about what Jesus Christ will be like during the Second Coming.

how often do we consider and remember Jesus is coming back in glory and power?

He shall return as He ascended

Many of us have varied images of Jesus that carry us throughout our lives. Different people see Jesus as different races, different nationalities, different sizes and shapes, different cosmetic features, and different ages. Images of Jesus have transcended every culture and race the world over. With so many different images of Jesus, how will He look when He returns?

In Acts 1:6-11, we receive poignant words: *Then they gathered around Him and asked Him, 'Lord, are You at this time going to restore the kingdom to Israel?' He said to them: 'It is not for you to know the times or dates the Father has set by His own authority. But you will receive power when the Holy Spirit comes on you; and you will be My witnesses in Jerusalem, and in all Judea and Samaria, and to the ends of the earth.' After He said this, He was taken up before their very eyes, and a cloud hid Him from their sight. They were looking intently up into the sky as He was going, when suddenly two men dressed in white stood beside them. 'Men of Galilee,' they said, "Why do you stand here looking into the sky? This same Jesus, Who has been taken from you into heaven, will come back in the same way you have seen Him go into heaven."* In this one passage, we learn a lot about the return of Jesus Christ. The first thing we learn is that He will indeed come again. While we do not know when that time will be, as it is at the Father's choosing, we do have full assurance He shall return unto us. The Second Coming was not the resurrection, as these words were spoken after the resurrection. Jesus will be back, as made in His promise, and not figuratively. If He is to return as they saw Him ascend, He is not going to be returning as a ghost or mere spiritual presence. He will look as He did and be just as real as He was back then. Jesus will return and we shall see Him again, and He shall again stand upon the earth.

Even though we don't know exactly how Jesus looked because there were no cameras in the first century, there are many indications we have as to His physical appearance. We can say, with assurance, Jesus will not

---

KEY VERSE: HEBREWS 9:28

So Christ was sacrificed once to take away the sins of many; and He will appear a second time, not to bear sin, but to bring salvation to those who are waiting for Him.

return to earth as a baby. Hebrews 9:28 says, *So Christ was sacrificed once to take away the sins of many; and He will appear a second time, not to bear sin, but to bring salvation to those who are waiting for Him.* As comforting as "Christmas Jesus" may be to many, that specific imagery of Christ does not apply to the Second Coming or how Christ will look or be when He returns.

Contrary to the popular images we have of Christ, He wasn't a blonde-hair, blue-eyed European, nor was Jesus of African descent. Jesus was of Sematic descent, which meant He had olive-toned skin, dark hair, and dark eyes. As that was His appearance upon ascension, it's reasonable to suggest He will still bear that resemblance somewhat upon His return. Revelation 1:12-16 describes Christ in the following way: *I turned around to see the voice that was speaking to me. And when I turned I saw seven golden lampstands, and among the lampstands was someone like a Son of Man, dressed in a robe reaching down to His feet and with a golden sash around His chest. The hair on His head was white like wool, as white as snow, and His eyes were like blazing fire. His feet were like bronze glowing in a furnace, and his voice was like the sound of rushing waters. In His right hand he held seven stars, and coming out of His mouth was a sharp, double-edged sword. His face was like the sun shining in all its brilliance.* Clearly Jesus Christ is returning in power and great glory!

Identifying Jesus

People have believed the Second Coming would happen in their lifetime for over one thousand years. By mistaking signs of their times, many of these people have been misled into believing other individuals were Jesus in the Second Coming. As we know from earlier in this article that Jesus shall return as He ascended, we can trust that Jesus will not return in the body of a different person. The Bible, in fact, warns us against Christ counterfeits that will come, claiming to be Jesus, but in fact, be sent by Satan for deception: *At that time if anyone says to you, 'Look, here is the Messiah!' or, 'Look, there he is!' do not believe it. For false messiahs and false prophets will appear and perform signs and wonders to deceive, if possible, even the elect.* (Mark 13:21-22) Clearly, we need to beware those who claim to be Jesus, the Christ, or some sort of concoction of Jesus in a human person. In the past two hundred years alone, people have believed Jesus "returned" in the form of a Persian charlatan, an elderly Korean man, a Hispanic counterfeit, and a necromancer - only to name a few. There are so many who come in the name of Christ, going as far as claiming to be Him, that we can never be too alert to prevent deception.

The reality of people trying to imitate Christ, versus other religious figures, should give us a keen sight to the truth present in His life, death, and resurrection. It also makes us keenly aware of His prophetic words and the true impact He has had on humanity. These false individuals also point us to a greater reality and bigger spiritual picture: *But in those days, following that distress, the sun will be darkened, and the moon will not give its light; the stars will fall from the sky, and the heavenly bodies will be shaken.' At that time people will see the Son of Man coming in clouds with great power and glory. And He will send His angels and gather His elect from the four winds, from the ends of the earth to the ends of the heavens.* (Mark 13:23-27) Seeing the rise of people who claim to be Christ, but are not, is a sign that the return of Jesus is in process and will come very soon.

Knowing the process and prophecies of the Savior helps us to recognize Him, all the more, upon His return. What keys exist that help us to better identify Him at His second coming?

Notable factors of the second coming

The same passage, mentioned above, states that Jesus shall come with the clouds, in great power and glory. This tells us the return of the Lord shall be a grand arrival, where He is seen in the clouds as a Ruler, King, Priest, and Prophet. He is returning not alone, but with His angels as well. This is to be no small event! It is not as simple as birth and life, nor as simple as just being a good teacher. This is one notable advance!

Jesus' return has the distinct air of royalty. In ancient times, much as today, heads of state and other dignitaries never travelled on their own. Jesus' return with angels of heaven, trumpeter's fanfare, and a gathering of His people shows forth a true people, aware of Who He is and prepared for His coming.

At the same time, Revelation 1:7 tells us, *"Look, he is coming with the clouds,"* and *"every eye will see Him, even those who pierced Him"; and all peoples on earth "will mourn because of Him." So shall it be! Amen.* EVERYONE will know Jesus has returned. It won't be a secret, there won't be time to rewind, but EVERYONE will see our Lord and Savior returning in power and judgment. There will be no fringe group followings! Everyone will know of His return and that He has returned, especially as other events unfold making His presence even more clear.

Jesus as judge

Most people prefer to regard Jesus as an infant because they do not like to think of Him as a Judge. Jesus is returning to judge all people (Micah 4:3). Revelation 20:4-6 tells us: *I saw thrones on which were seated those*

> **AUTHOR'S REFLECTIONS**
>
> We often hear details as pertain to the Second Coming through the eyes of instructors and theologians who have been influenced by different theories and philosophies of faith throughout history. The catch is with these different teachings that not all of them relate to a true understanding of Biblical knowledge. If we are to be people who want to know what to expect when Jesus returns, it is often better to unplug much of the dramatic rhetoric we hear and start looking at the Scriptures. While it's true that the Bible doesn't give many specific details, it does let us know what to think and what to watch for.

who had been given authority to judge. And I saw the souls of those who had been beheaded because of their testimony about Jesus and because of the word of God. They had not worshiped the beast or its image and had not received its mark on their foreheads or their hands. They came to life and reigned with Christ a thousand years. (The rest of the dead did not come to life until the thousand years were ended.) This is the first resurrection. Blessed and holy are those who share in the first resurrection. The second death has no power over them, but they will be priests of God and of Christ and will reign with Him for a thousand years. Jesus, as the Resurrection and the Life, is qualified to serve as judge for dispute and sin alike. Everyone will be accountable for their deeds, good or bad. His justice will be swift, powerful, and exact. There will be no questions or do-overs; but the clear reality of our lives and His influence (or lack thereof over us).

In this passage, we also see another relevant reason why God's people must recognize Christ: they shall be appointed as judges with Him. If we are busy looking to the wrong things or wrong images of Christ, we can't be His people prepared to rule and reign with Him!

Jesus as warrior

The last main way we see Jesus in the second coming is as a warrior. To some, a loving Savior and a warrior are a contradiction, not to mention scary or intimidating. As we fight for those we love, so too Jesus fights for us against our enemy, Satan. We have no reason to fear Jesus' warrior stance if we are in right standing with Him, ready to fight alongside in battle. In the Kingdom of God, we are not just called to serve our Savior passively, but actively, and recognize the power in spiritual warfare. As we are called to battle, so too is Jesus.

One of the most often discussed, debated, and controversial battle gatherings ever to occur in history is prophesied to occur when Jesus returns. Revelation 16:12-16 tells us: *The sixth angel poured out his bowl* on the great river Euphrates, and its water was dried up to prepare the way for the kings from the East. Then I saw three impure spirits that looked like frogs; they came out of the mouth of the dragon, out of the mouth of the beast and out of the mouth of the false prophet. They are demonic spirits that perform signs, and they go out to the kings of the whole world, to gather them for the battle on the great day of God Almighty. 'Look, I come like a thief! Blessed is the one who stays awake and remains clothed, so as not to go naked and be shamefully exposed.' Then they gathered the kings together to the place that in Hebrew is called Armageddon. When the world comes to fight, Jesus will stand, ready to rise to the challenge.

Knowing the Savior

For thousands of years, cultures, religions, and societies have portrayed Jesus in certain ways. We can see Jesus in any stage of development, at any age, on earth, and in heaven. The image of Jesus has been impressed upon holidays, church walls, pictures, statues, and beyond. In more modern times, Jesus' image has been used to sell a pop-culture type phenomenon on T-shirts, pins, skateboards, music videos, and other aspects of media. While I truly think it's fantastic we see Jesus in so many different ways and in so many different places, wearing a picture of Jesus on a T-shirt or standing on His head while skateboarding doesn't indicate a true knowledge of Him. Every year at Christmastime, the world makes Jesus a lawn decoration and an excuse to over-spend, without truly coming to know Him or the power of His resurrection.

When Jesus returns, whether or not we know Him will be a focal point. It is essential we recognize His humanity and divinity in the fullness of all He is. No longer will He be a baby, no longer will He return to suffer for sins, and no longer will He tolerate the nonsense so rampant in this world today. If we are a people recognizing our times and preparing to meet our Savior, why don't we take some time to know Him? Jesus is a returning King, Savior, Judge, Warrior, and true Friend. As we study the Word and commit ourselves to Him, we come to a deeper love and understanding of Him and His nature.

Jesus is coming soon...Are you ready?

Apostle Marino outside of Sanctuary Apostolic Fellowship (later to become Sanctuary International Fellowship Tabernacle – SIFT) in Raleigh, North Carolina (February 2016)

3 WISDOM CRIES OUT
(Volume 9, No. 1 – January 2010)

When most of us were young, we heard of our elders as "wise and old" men and women who had acquired much wisdom from their life experiences. Wisdom was something taught to be acquired from living a long time, passed down through stories which started out with "When I was young..." We didn't give much attention to the nature of wisdom, what it was, or how it was acquired, save that it was something we couldn't have because we weren't very old.

As we got older, we've all seen our learnings of wisdom fall short. Older people don't always seem so wise anymore - and in truth, many younger people don't seem very wise, either. There are many experiences that don't seem to make us wise, only frustrated. Sometimes our experiences cause us more questions instead of less, and we don't always understand what our situations are about. It would be nice if wisdom came in a nice, neat, identifiable package....so why doesn't it?

It is true that God does not teach wisdom to fall on our heads or arrive one day on our doorstep. God also does not promise that experience gains wisdom. Even though many people may go through experiences and come out wiser, that is their choice. Many go through trying or difficult situations and do not come out with any wisdom. We also learn, as we come to study the Word, that wisdom is not an acquisition based on age or years of living.

If everything we've ever thought or learned about wisdom is false, then what of wisdom is true?

Wisdom is an understanding gained from living deeply in the Lord and recognizing His ways in our experiences. It is when we finally come to the place where we recognize it isn't all about our understanding or human knowledge applied to situations, and that God's ways are truly different and deeper than our own. When we come to live life from this perspective, it gives us a certain richness to have enough good sense and judgment to know when results will be beneficial or harmful. Where does it lie? Where do we find it?

Job's forty-year experience of suffering and difficulty caused him to ponder many deep questions about life and experience. If we examine the book of Job in detail, we can note that much of his search examined the issue of wisdom: what it was, where it lies, and how it is acquired. Job 28:1-28 gives a powerful and passionate examination of wisdom: *There is a mine for silver and a place where gold is refined. Iron is taken from the earth, and copper is smelted from ore. Man puts an end to the darkness; he searches the farthest recesses for ore in the blackest darkness. Far from where people dwell he cuts a shaft, in places forgotten by the foot of man; far from men he dangles and sways. The earth, from which food comes, is transformed below as by fire; sapphires come from its rocks, and its dust contains nuggets of gold. No bird of prey knows that hidden path, no falcon's eye has seen it. Proud beasts do not set foot on it, and no lion prowls there. Man's hand assaults the flinty rock and lays bare the roots of the mountains. He tunnels through the rock; his eyes see all its treasures. He searches the sources of the rivers and brings hidden things to light. 'But where can wisdom be found? Where does understanding dwell? Man does not comprehend its worth; it cannot be found in the land of the living. The deep says, 'It is not in me'; the sea says, 'It is not with me.' It cannot be bought with the finest gold, nor can its price be weighed in silver. It cannot be bought with the gold of Ophir, with precious onyx or sapphires. Neither gold nor crystal can compare with it, nor can it be had for jewels of gold. Coral and jasper are not worthy of mention; the price of wisdom is beyond rubies. The topaz of Cush cannot compare with it; it cannot be bought with pure gold. "Where then does wisdom come from? Where does understanding dwell? It is hidden from the eyes of every living thing, concealed even from the birds of the air. Destruction and Death say, 'Only a rumor of it has reached our ears.' God*

> **BEHIND THE ARTICLE**
>
> Wisdom is one of my favorite topics, so this turned out to be an easy article for me to tackle. Looking at the depth of writing the Bible offers on wisdom helped me see more of why it is so important for us to seek it out as believers.

understands the way to it and He alone knows where it dwells, for He views the ends of the earth and sees everything under the heavens. When He established the force of the wind and measured out the waters, when He made a decree for the rain and a path for the thunderstorm, then He looked at wisdom and appraised it; He confirmed it and tested it. And He said to man, 'The fear of the Lord—that is wisdom, and to shun evil is understanding.'

Obviously, the search for wisdom is not just important, it is essential! In looking at Job 28, we see not just Job's struggle, but the answer to what he seeks. Wisdom lies in God and having reverential awe of our Creator. The more we come to know God and the deeper we develop relationship with Him, the more wisdom we will acquire. If we remain in God, God remains in us, and we develop divine insight into the situations which we face and experience.

One relevant thing we learn about wisdom is that, as with all things in God, we do not just have to find wisdom on our own. God reaches out to us with wisdom, and it is ours as we diligently seek Him. Proverbs 8:1-11 tells us how intently wisdom seeks us as we seek it: *Does not wisdom call out? Does not understanding raise her voice? On the heights along the way, where the paths meet, she takes her stand; beside the gates leading into the city, at the entrances, she cries aloud: 'To you, O men, I call out; I raise my voice to all mankind. You who are simple, gain prudence; you who are foolish, gain understanding. Listen, for I have worthy things to say; I open my lips to speak what is right. My mouth speaks what is true, for my lips detest wickedness. All the words of my mouth are just; none of them is crooked or perverse. To the discerning all of them are right; they are faultless to those who have knowledge. Choose my instruction instead of silver, knowledge rather than choice gold, for wisdom is more precious than rubies, and nothing you desire can compare with her.'* It's apparent that if we can only seek one thing from God, we need to seek greater wisdom because discovering wisdom leads us to a more profound level of faith and living.

KEY VERSE: PROVERBS 8:1 AND 11

Does not wisdom call out? Does not understanding raise her voice?
...For wisdom is more precious than rubies, and nothing you desire can compare with her.

Why is wisdom so important?

One may inquire as to why the obtaining of wisdom is so essential. As wisdom is described as being better than rubies in Proverbs 8, we can see it has an immeasurable strength, purpose, and value. But why is wisdom so relevant? Isn't it better to not know things than to look with observation and have to make decisions and choices about things?

Many people today adopt the mentality that wisdom is simply not worth the hassle. Wisdom leads to knowing which leads to responsibility and too many do not want to deal with the hassle of having to make wise decisions and be responsible for actions. Such an end reaps destruction and negative life. As believers, we know wisdom is a part of God's design for an abundant life in Him. What are the reasons why wisdom is so important in the life of a believer?

The first reason is because wisdom helps us to know God and understand the ways of God better. While we will never come to a point where we fully understand God and His ways, wisdom sets us on a path where our choices reflect our desire to know God deeply.

As part of the first reason, the second ties in: wisdom is relevant because we are representatives of the goodness, love, mercy, and truth of God. If God acts in wisdom, surely part of our representation to the world must be a wise style of living and spiritual presentation.

A third reason why wisdom is so important is because wisdom leads to a better life. So often people's negative choices result from a lack of applied wisdom. When we don't learn from God, we don't learn from our circumstances. If we want to draw on the strength of God and stop repeating choices, behaviors, family patterns, old decisions, and negative ways of thinking and living, we need to learn about the precepts of wisdom to make better choices. Making better choices leads us to a better way and quality of life. Tired of all that old junk you keep carrying around? Try wisdom!

A fourth reason for the importance of wisdom is because wisdom displays maturity. Immature believers demand a great amount of time and attention to their needs. In the beginning, this is understandable, as new believers require teaching, support, and understanding from those around them as they begin to grow in faith. This should begin to change, however, as believers grow and develop wisdom and insight in their faith. Individuals who are excessively immature after years in faith are a drain on other believers and become a negative witness. Wisdom provides us with the stability to be consistent in our belief and grow in our faith despite our circumstances.

An unwise age

Foolishness and folly are often spoken to be the enemies of wisdom. It's no surprise to look around today and note that most people do not employ wisdom as they should, thus rendering an age of foolishness and folly. Improper decisions, poor judgment, and indecent behavior all demonstrate a total lack of wisdom among most of our society.

As mentioned earlier, many people simply do not want to take the time to develop wisdom and accept responsibility for making wise choices. The truth is that whether or not the foolish become wise, they remain accountable for their choices; the results for such choices, however, are quite different when the foolish refuse wisdom. Proverbs 8:35-36 makes the following truth come alive: *For whoever finds me finds life and receives favor from the LORD. But whoever fails to find me harms himself; all who hate me love death.* Destruction awaits those who live by foolishness and deny wisdom!

It can be difficult for those who work in developing wisdom to watch others exercise such poor choices. It is especially hard when the consequences of others' poor choices can affect the wise negatively. It is also difficult to watch individuals reap the consequences of living foolishly who we care about. The truth, however, is that even amidst this foolish age, God has a plan for the wise to develop even more wisdom. In Ecclesiastes 7:24-25, we get a new insight into the discovery of wisdom: *Whatever wisdom may be, it is far off and most profound—who can discover it? So I turned my mind to understand, to investigate and to search out wisdom and the scheme of things and to understand the stupidity of wickedness and the madness of folly.* The philosopher of Ecclesiastes believed wisdom was too difficult to find on its own, so he learned about it through observing wickedness and folly! By watching what not to do, he learned what to do. The same is true for us. Our purpose is not to be spirited out of the current age, but to continue to grow and gain wisdom by seeing examples all around us of folly and wickedness.

The example of Solomon

We know from Bible stories that Solomon was considered the wisest man who ever lived. What we don't often consider is that Solomon's birth did not occur under the wisest of circumstances. Solomon was the product of David's relationship with Bathsheba after David had her first husband killed. Likewise, the Bible shows Solomon's ascent to the throne was not without its controversy. Solomon had a lot ahead of him to confront and face as king, and he knew it. What was Solomon to seek to be a great king? 1 Kings 3:4-15 describes what he knew it would take to be great:

> **AUTHOR'S REFLECTIONS**
>
> The work of ministry requires a great deal of wisdom. Whether it's discerning spirits, figuring out how to handle a situation, or trying to get the rent on the building paid, ministry requires the minister to be extremely wise in all things. When we first ran this article, looking at wisdom from so many different perspectives challenged me to apply wisdom throughout my ministry in different ways. It still challenges me to do such today.

The king went to Gibeon to offer sacrifices, for that was the most important high place, and Solomon offered a thousand burnt offerings on that altar. At Gibeon the LORD appeared to Solomon during the night in a dream, and God said, 'Ask for whatever you want me to give You.' Solomon answered, 'You have shown great kindness to Your servant, my father David, because he was faithful to You and righteous and upright in heart. You have continued this great kindness to him and have given him a son to sit on his throne this very day. Now, O LORD my God, You have made Your servant king in place of my father David. But I am only a little child and do not know how to carry out my duties. Your servant is here among the people You have chosen, a great people, too numerous to count or number. So give Your servant a discerning heart to govern Your people and to distinguish between right and wrong. For who is able to govern this great people of Yours?' The Lord was pleased that Solomon had asked for this. So God said to him, "Since you have asked for this and not for long life or wealth for yourself, nor have asked for the death of your enemies but for discernment in administering justice, I will do what you have asked. I will give you a wise and discerning heart, so that there will never have been anyone like you, nor will there ever be. Moreover, I will give you what you have not asked for—both riches and honor—so that in your lifetime you will have no equal among kings. And if you walk in My ways and obey My statutes and commands as David your father did, I will give you a long life.' Then Solomon awoke—and he realized it had been a dream. Solomon's heart was right - he had it set that he needed to be a wise and discerning leader to bring good leadership unto God's people. We can see here that God also gave Solomon riches and honor as a result of his request for wisdom. God knew Solomon could be trusted with great things because wisdom was destined to be the foundation of his leadership.

What are you seeking God for? Many of us are seeking God for money, riches, fame, many followers, big churches, new cars, houses, and other things which are just that - things. The Bible does not tell us to seek after things, but after the Kingdom: *But seek first His Kingdom and His righteousness, and all these things will be given to you as well.* (Matthew

6:33) Seeking wisdom is an essential part of seeking the Kingdom of God! Instead of seeking things, we need to seek more of the face of God and understand Him better, thus walking in the precepts and truth of God in a greater way!

Solomon shows us the secret of impacting other lives does not lie in having a lot of assorted stuff, but in walking, living, and leading in wisdom. His is an example to raise up and consider as we go through our times and truly seek greater wisdom to handle every circumstance, deep question or thought, and every individual Kingdom life we come to effect.

Recognizing the importance of daily wisdom

Every one of us is given the same twenty-four-hour period of time in a day. In that period of time, we all are given the same ability to seek God and live by wisdom. Psalm 90:12 provides us with words to live by: *Teach us to number our days aright, that we may gain a heart of wisdom.* If we will only put God first and seek His Kingdom, we will find wisdom will abound in our lives. Wisdom doesn't live far off in Tibet or require hours of painful physical discipline. As we number our days, spending our time focused on that which is important and spending less time on that which is not important, we come to develop better spiritual insights into our daily living and the choices we make. God has not made wisdom impossible to find, nor has He made wisdom ridiculously impossible to obtain. If we truly seek to make a Kingdom impact, we will find wisdom seated in the heart of God. Wisdom will thus reveal itself to us as we live in the center of God's will. Obedience remains key, as does spiritual discernment, in every situation we face.

Want to become wise? Be a radically obedient child of God, trusting Him in all things!

Apostle Marino preaching in Dunn, North Carolina (January 2010)

4 Paradigm Shift
(Volume 12, No. 1 – January/February 2013)

When I was in school, radical changes were constantly being made to the school curriculum due to political influences affecting education. My own kindergarten teacher declared study of the alphabet to be "boring" and therefore taught the letters of the alphabet in a crazy, nonsensical order, starting with the letter C. We did not have phonics education until I was in second grade as first the subject was removed, and then it was put back. Mathematics were taught all sorts of strange ways, with heavy emphasis on algebraic training and less on basic concepts. New things were being tried and then removed, and older things likewise were removed and put back. Looking back over this time, I am amazed that any of us could read or function educationally at all.

What I did not know at the time was that we were caught right in the middle of a changing paradigm, one in which education was shifting from being educational to political. I was a part of a change that I didn't facilitate and didn't understand. Even though the signs were there that such a change was imminent, I was unaware because of my level of understanding.

Whether or not we are consciously aware, we are all a part of a paradigm or several paradigms. Throughout our lives, the paradigm to which we ascribe often shifts, changes, or becomes new through a process of selecting one paradigm over another. The word "paradigm" is frequently invoked to describe a concept and the method by which that concept is executed. For example, "paradigm" is frequently used to describe thought in medical and psychiatric communities. In this context, a paradigm refers to a theory pertaining to treatment, diagnosis, and ethics. In education, a paradigm refers to an educational style, method, or teaching implementation. In religion, a paradigm refers to a belief system, pattern of ritual, or regulation. There are many other ways that "paradigm" is used: to describe a popular movement, philosophy, idea, concept, method, or ideology. A paradigm can be positive or negative, as the concept of a paradigm is neutral in its application. Because of its broad use, many people use it to describe many different things and in many different contexts. The concept behind the paradigm, however, remains the same.

In the spiritual realm, religion has created a paradigm in terms of how people think Christianity, its leaders, and its members should operate, function, believe, and behave. The religious paradigm created has created dishonest people, anger at God, hostility toward faith, a worldly spirit within the church, and chaos among those who call themselves "Christians." It is not uncommon to find so-called believers behaving just as worldly as non-believers, contributing to the end times shifting of events without perpetual end.

The world itself will continually follow through paradigm after paradigm until the return of Jesus Christ. What, however, for the church? Are we to be continually changing with the world? Or is it time, once and for all, for the church to shift to a paradigm which will never shift again?

> **BEHIND THE ARTICLE**
>
> I had wanted to do an article on "paradigm shift" for quite some time prior to the publication of this work. As an updated version of an older article I published in *Power For Today* that I wanted to update, *Paradigm Shift* came at a point in my life and ministry where I was undergoing a great shift, as I entered the beginning of a season that truly threw off my entire paradigm. It brought necessary change, but with that change came a lot of tumult I did not expect.

A voice crying in the wilderness

The spiritual situation which exists today is not all that different from the one that existed in the first century. Religious legislation had people bound, thinking their salvation rested in obedience to many rules and rulers who interpreted the law. Religious people of that time also believed the political system which oversaw secular government was the true reason why their people could not worship or obey God like they should. It was one of those situations where the people who claimed to be godly blamed the fact that they were not as godly as they should be on everyone else, and they would be like they should be when outside circumstances changed. While some did genuinely try to follow God through the rules in place, the majority of leaders and lazy people blamed their lack of true spirituality on everyone else around them.

Sound familiar? Truly we can see from Bible prophecy the last days are upon us: *But mark this: There will be terrible times in the last days. People will be lovers of themselves, lovers of money, boastful, proud, abusive, disobedient to their parents, ungrateful, unholy, without love, unforgiving, slanderous, without self-control, brutal, not lovers of the good, treacherous, rash, conceited, lovers of pleasure rather than lovers of God— having a form of godliness but denying its power. Have nothing to do with them.* Biblical prophecy itself shows the end times as a constant paradigm shift, with people shifting from bad to worse in all areas of their lives. The behavior of the world, despite any attempts to better social thinking, will increase in its destructiveness and eventually cave in on itself at the return of Jesus Christ.

One of the most prominent aspects of these times is the last mentioned characteristic of the day, more or less tying in all the behaviors together: people who have a form of godliness but deny its power. In reality, many people today claim to live faithfully, adhere to a seemingly religious pattern of belief, and yet deny true godliness over the self-righteous paradigm of religion. As if the world does not have enough problems, there is the contention of religious legalism created to cause confusion, disunity, and self-righteousness in the church. There is no question that a new, fixed, and lasting paradigm is needed. But what?

Even though we don't often think of it in this way, John the Baptist came, proclaiming a new paradigm. He was anti-establishment, counterculture, and came with a message calling people to change their ways and accept those of God rather than conventional paradigms. Matthew 3:1-6 tells of the essence of John's personage, mission, and calling: *In those days there appeared John the Baptist, preaching in the Wilderness (Desert) of Judea and saying, Repent (think differently; change your mind, regretting your sins and changing your conduct), for the kingdom of heaven is at hand. This is he who was mentioned by the prophet Isaiah when he said, The voice of one crying in the wilderness (shouting in the desert), Prepare the road for the Lord, make His highways straight (level, direct). This same John's garments were made of camel's*

KEY VERSE: MATTHEW 3:1-2

In those days there appeared John the Baptist, preaching in the Wilderness (Desert) of Judea and saying, Repent (think differently; change your mind, regretting your sins and changing your conduct), for the Kingdom of heaven is at hand. (AMPC) *hair, and he wore a leather girdle about his waist; and his food was locusts and wild honey. Then Jerusalem and all Judea and all the country round about the Jordan went out to him; and they were baptized in the Jordan by him, confessing their sins.* (AMPC)

We all know that John's purpose was to prepare the way for Jesus, but do we consider what that calling actually meant? It was John's purpose to proclaim something in total opposition to the historical paradigm in which he lived and proclaim the complete opposite of what was popular at the time. John was a literal "voice of one," the only voice recognizing the signs of the time and embracing the task of preparing hearts and minds for the coming of Christ's ministry by changing those hearts and minds. By setting people on the course for Christ, John changed their paradigm forever.

A voice not without opposition

Many today ascribe to the belief that we can't be Christian without a Christian-based secular government. This is a truly nonsensical argument as the first century believers never lived under Christian government and their faith spread rather than diminished. The real truth behind such a mentality is that many people today don't want to stand against the establishment as they are afraid to be different.

The essence of the Christian call is to be different. Accepting God's paradigm versus the world's paradigm means that we won't look, act, or interact as the world does while we are still here. Instead of shying back, however, a true recognizer of a paradigm shift will stand up and confront the current paradigm in defense of God's Kingdom: *But when he saw many of the Pharisees and Sadducees coming for baptism, he said to them, You brood of vipers! Who warned you to flee and escape from the wrath and indignation [of God against disobedience] that is coming? Bring forth fruit that is consistent with repentance [let your lives prove your change of heart]; and do not presume to say to yourselves, We have Abraham for our forefather; for I tell you, God is able to raise up descendants for Abraham from these stones! And already the ax is lying at the root of the trees; every tree therefore that does not bear good fruit is cut down and thrown into the fire.* (Matthew 3:7-10, AMPC) Clearly, those who come for religious reasons are seeking to cause trouble for the Kingdom advance and stop the shift which is to occur. As the herald moves, calling to truth, the world will always be ready, willing, and able to intervene in the change.

Undermining authority

One of the reasons why Christians are advised to submit to civil authorities and governments is because God's ultimate paradigm shift completely and totally uproots conventional systems. In being a Christian, one is accepting the power of Christ as supreme over every worldly power and authority. This is in direct opposition to what secular authorities believe about themselves. In essence, this same fact is true about religious authorities as well.

It's not a big secret that authority dislikes challenge. People of power respond very poorly to others that come along and challenge what they have established and set up because it threatens their very rule. With every paradigm shift comes a change in the leaders, rulers, and founders. Shifting to God's paradigm indicates we no longer see the rulers of traditional paradigms in the same way we used to. As paradigms always point to the ones who established the set foundation for thinking and action, it is obvious that those in God's paradigm will truly point to Christ, the appointed One to lead this shift. Continuing in Matthew 3, verses 11-12 exhibits how John handled this issue: *I indeed baptize you in (with) water because of repentance [that is, because of your changing your minds for the better, heartily amending your ways, with abhorrence of your past sins]. But He Who is coming after me is mightier than I, Whose sandals I am not worthy or fit to take off or carry; He will baptize you with the Holy Spirit and with fire. His winnowing fan (shovel, fork) is in His hand, and He will thoroughly clear out and clean His threshing floor and gather and store His wheat in His barn, but the chaff He will burn up with fire that cannot be put out.* (AMPC) Clearly when one has accepted God's paradigm they stop shifting between people and pointing to the One Who baptizes us with the Holy Spirit and with fire!

Differences in the paradigms

Each existing paradigm has its own unique stamp which separates it from other paradigms. How can we identify people in the Kingdom paradigm versus those in worldly ones?

- **Different beliefs** - No matter how neutral the world systems claim to be, all paradigms hold to belief systems that, either directly or indirectly, pay homage to someone or something. The fruit of such belief manifests in the paradigm's shift that following God is about how things appear on the outside. Any true representative of Christ recognizes that what we do when no one sees us is just as important as what we do in the public presentation of faith. We must make sure our behavior is consistent across the board, to everyone we encounter. 2 Thessalonians 2:13-15 gives to us a gentle reminder of the importance in maintaining different beliefs: *But we ought always to thank God for you, brothers loved by the Lord, because* *from the beginning God chose you to be saved through the sanctifying work of the Spirit and through belief in the truth. He called you to this through our gospel, that you might share in the glory of our Lord Jesus Christ. So then, brothers, stand firm and hold to the teachings we passed on to you, whether by word of mouth or by letter.* Those who are in God's paradigm know what they believe and must live by it. Those in alternate paradigms may know what they believe, but their beliefs are constantly in flux and changing, creating confusion.

> **AUTHOR'S REFLECTIONS**
>
> As much as many of us complain that things happen slowly, very few of us genuinely like change because change signifies great shake-ups in our lives. When it comes to the radical shifting of a paradigm, we need to be ready – and prepared – to have our entire world shaken up, changed, and then put back down so we can become something other than we are right now.

- **Different speech** - Luke 6:45 gives us a profound revelation about our use of words: *The good man brings good things out of the good stored up in his heart, and the evil man brings evil things out of the evil stored up in his heart. For out of the overflow of his heart his mouth speaks.* Some people are chronically negative in their speech, no matter what happens to them. Other people take the Lord's name in vain or are foul in their speech. Then there are those who are quick to spout off doctrine at any chance they get. When you speak, what comes out? How someone speaks is very revealing of their paradigm. When we speak differently than other people, constantly reflecting the glory of God in our representation of truth, we show forth that we are a part of a radically different paradigm than those of this world.

- **Different priorities** - Where do your priorities lie? It's amazing to note how many people have no money to buy food or pay the rent but have money to buy cigarettes and beer. It's not uncommon to find people who cry poverty and claim they have no money for the Kingdom of God and yet they have money for lavish and expensive trips or gifts during holiday seasons. Where are priorities lie indicate where our allegiance lies and, by proxy, who is the center of our paradigm. 2 Corinthians 5:9 says, *So we make it our goal to please*

Him, whether we are at home in the body or away from it. Is pleasing God your first priority in all things? If it's not, you may need to recognize it's time to shift your paradigm!

- **Different precepts** - Different paradigms hold to different core precepts which unite those who abide by its way of thinking. One core precept of worldly precepts is that they revolve around certain concepts that often change, at least on the surface. People following worldly paradigms often struggle with grave unhappiness, difficult moral questions and situations, and a general inconsistency when it comes to honesty and integrity. In contrast, Psalm 19:8 gives insight into following the precepts of God: *The precepts of the LORD are right, giving joy to the heart. The commands of the LORD are radiant, giving light to the eyes.* Are you living by precepts that bring joy to the heart and light to your eyes? If not, no matter what your claims, your paradigm may truly be to blame!

A powerful future

Even though the situations of this world are not going to get better, God is giving us the opportunity to hear and heed the call to repent, change our ways, turn around, and follow Him. We always have the opportunity to heed the call and follow God's paradigm unto life and light. While theories may come and go as fleeting, fading concepts, the truth of God is eternal and brings us into a deeper place of trust and love with our Creator. As the world winds down by continuously following its destructive courses, the people of God sustain their lives with grace and peace.

The question becomes one of willingness to lay aside the ways of this world, admit they do not work, and focus on further to the ways of God and His eternal paradigm which will not fail or falter. The choice is ours, to hear the voice of one calling out and heed the eternal words or to remain in worldly thinking. Even if you are somewhere between the world and God, it's time to set both feet firmly in the Kingdom and live in a singular paradigm that leads to life, love, and eternity in Christ.

Apostle Marino ministering in Danville, Virginia (June 2015)

5 Lord, Teach Me To Pray!
(Volume 8, Number 8—August 2010)

When I first decided to write about prayer, I immediately remembered being young and in traditional church. The church I belonged to back then engaged in prayer in the same way it had since around the sixteenth century: prayers were read by the priest, who read them from a book, and then the congregation would respond with a tired "amen" as soon as he finished speaking. Prayers were always formal and never spontaneous. One of the cornerstones of our religious education was learning the church's textbook prayers. It seemed as if there was one of these rehearsed prayers for every event under the sun. Lost something? Send up a signal to St. Anthony. Having trouble with your children? Mary was the key to getting that issue resolved. Have a hopeless case? Drop St. Jude a line. A prayer consisting of many words and several implications had been penned and printed on small cards for every situation. We were told how we could pray, how we should pray, the posture we should adopt for prayer, when we should pray, and even what we should pray for. Every aspect of our prayer lives was penned and detailed by someone else, either living or dead, who may or may not have had the slightest idea what we were going through and what we were facing in our modern times. Prayer wasn't a communication with God, it was a scripted rehearsal of lines pre-prepared to gain attention by ethereal beings who had ascended to godhood.

It's no surprise that once I became a Christian, I had no idea how to pray or what prayer really was. I thought prayer was this big formal event scripted by a book. In looking to other Christians around me, I didn't find much help in learning the correct paths to prayer. Others around me were poor models of proper prayer due to their own religious backgrounds. The vast majority of people I met in those early years had a similarly uncomfortable and awkward approach to prayer. It was as if our prayer lives were completely stumped without a book in front of us to define what a prayer was.

> **BEHIND THE ARTICLE**
>
> I was initially concerned that doing a basic cover article on prayer would insult my readership, because the way I approached prayer was very basic. It turned out to be my most popular article and our best-selling edition to date.

I think it's safe to say many people are confused about prayer in one way or another. Whether it's misunderstanding what prayer is itself or misunderstanding how to pray, most do not pray correctly, according to Scriptural guidelines. Not surprisingly, they do not receive satisfaction in their prayer lives or with the answers God sends to them. How can we pray effectively and Scripturally to receive the results we seek?

Confused about prayer

Confusion about prayer isn't new. In fact, religion has been creating confusion about prayer for well over two thousand years. In the first century, the disciples of Jesus came unto Him, saying, *Lord, teach us to pray, as John also taught his disciples.* (Luke 11:1) The mere fact that they came unto Christ, their Master and Teacher, to inquire about prayer indicates they were unsure how to pray themselves. The Scriptures give us indication of common religious methods of prayer employed in the first century. Interestingly enough, many of them are still in use today: pray long, pray wordy, and pray very publicly. Matthew 6:5-8 says: *And when thou prayest, thou shalt not be as the hypocrites are: for they love to pray standing in the synagogues and in the corners of the streets, that they may be seen of men. Verily I say unto you, They have their reward. But thou, when thou prayest, enter into thy closet, and when thou hast shut thy door, pray to thy Father which is in secret; and thy Father which seeth in secret shall reward thee openly. But when ye pray, use not vain repetitions, as the heathen do: for they think that they shall be heard for their much speaking. Be not ye therefore like unto them: for your Father knoweth what things ye have need of, before ye ask Him.* (KJV) Jesus begins to bring clarity to the matter of prayer by establishing why people are confused about prayer:

because when approached with a religious attitude, prayer becomes a display of religiousness rather than a communication with God. This is the first, and most common reason, people find prayer ineffective: prayer becomes all about their display, and not about God. If we desire a powerful prayer life, we have to pray with a right spirit. Until we get the spirit right within ourselves, we will have difficulty and confusion on matters of prayer. Jesus also encourages us to spend our private devotional time alone with God. Does this mean we cannot pray as part of a public worship service? No, Jesus isn't saying that. What Jesus is telling us, however, is that we must make sure we spend devotional time with the Father, void of distractions, displays, and other people, to receive a direct word from Him. Prayer as a communion with God isn't much good if it is littered with distractions. Public prayer is good and serves a purpose, but personal prayer serves a very different purpose that is frequently overlooked. If we desire to know how to pray correctly, we must pray privately with God.

What to pray

Another key to effective prayer is to limit word usage. We have no need to make a big display of our prayers, nor do we have to talk on and on excessively because God knows our needs. When praying, we ask God in faith, knowing He will provide us with an answer. Talking excessively de-centers our focus and blocks our ability to hear from God as we pray. Littering prayer with many words doesn't make it more effective, it just makes it long. God won't hear you any clearer if you try to talk fancy or be impressive; in fact, many prayers in the Scriptures have been short and to the point and were quite effective. So, when we pray, if it's not about using a lot of words, what should we pray? Jesus answers this in Matthew 6:9-13: *After this manner therefore pray ye: Our Father which art in heaven, Hallowed be Thy Name. Thy Kingdom come, Thy will be done in earth, as it is in heaven. Give us this day our daily bread. And forgive us our debts, as we forgive our debtors. And lead us not into temptation, but deliver us from evil: For Thine is the Kingdom, and the power, and the glory, for ever. Amen.* (KJV) Jesus makes prayer easy for us here, outlining a few major areas for us to cover in our prayers. If we examine these areas, we can be assured an effective and joyful prayer life. They are: 1) Praise the Name of God, 2) Pray for Kingdom matters, 3) Pray for necessities, 4) Pray for forgiveness, 5) Pray against temptations, and 6) Pray for all that

---

KEY VERSE: LUKE 11:1

Lord, teach us to pray, as John also taught his disciples.

belongs to God.

1. Praise the Name of God

I believe all effective prayer begins by praising God for all He is and in all His power, and praising God in His Name through the Name of His Son, Jesus Christ is the most effective way we can praise God for all He is. I am reminded of the words of 1 Chronicles 29:13: *Now therefore, our God, we thank Thee, and praise Thy glorious Name.* (KJV) To praise the Name of God means we praise all God has ever done, ever will do, and is now doing, even if we don't know what that may be. To praise the Name of God is to praise His supremacy and His grandeur, and to reaffirm our need for Him. Praising God is the cornerstone to prayer because through it we identify Him in glory and ourselves in humility. Praising God's Name can be done through song, through reading Scriptures praising His Name, or even just speaking words of praise to God for all He has done.

2. Pray for Kingdom matters

Do you remember to pray for matters affecting the Kingdom of God? Many of us don't, being overly caught up in problems we are facing or needs we have. Jesus instructs us, however, in Matthew 6:33: *But seek ye first the Kingdom of God, and His righteousness; and all these things shall be added unto you.* (KJV) When praying for matters, Kingdom issues must come first because the advance of God's Kingdom is our first priority. If we seek first God's Kingdom, we can trust that God will take care of all our needs in Christ Jesus and we can go on as faithful stewards with the Gospel, living our lives every day according to Kingdom principles.

3. Pray for necessities

Sometimes I think if one more Christian tells me they are believing God for a new car…or a fur coat…or a boat…or a bigger house…I am going to lose it. This intense desire Christians have for things shows a blurring between understanding want and need. Most Christians you meet are very in touch with what they want, and they are quick to tell both you and God what they think He should give to them. God, however, asks that we are more in touch with need than want. Our first priority, when praying for matters pertaining to life, should be need rather than want. In focusing first on need and then want, it creates a different outlook on life. Knowledge of need keeps us from greed and from excessive want. It provides us with the grace to make ourselves aware of a need for moderation when applicable.

This issue, however, raises an important question: what do we really need in our life? Jesus gives us an example of need in Matthew 6: our daily bread, or physical nourishment. Rightly this could be classified as a statement to cover all our regular needs for survival. We need food, we need shelter, we need water, we need clothing and shoes, we need to have basic needs met that we may continue in our callings and be productive with them, we need companionship and fellowship, we need emotional health and mental stability, and we need love. Beyond that, all things unnecessary for living become wants. It's not wrong to have wants or to pray that God gives us certain things; that is not wrong at all. But it is certainly wrong to want so much that we lose sight of need when so many of this world live in a perpetual state of unmet needs. Luke 12:30 reveals an important truth we must always keep mind in prayer: *...Your Father knoweth that ye have need of these things.* (KJV) In prayer, we cast our needs upon God, knowing that He shall meet all our needs according to His riches and glory in Christ Jesus.

4. Pray for forgiveness

Forgiveness is one of those topics we can't hear enough about. As we go through life, forgiveness will be something we will continually require, both from others and for others, not to mention the forgiveness we need from God. Forgiveness is a primary element of prayer as it is the very foundation of our faith. We can forgive because we know we are forgiven by God through Christ. Why not make forgiveness a daily practice? Every day, ask God to forgive you for what you have done wrong and also ask God to forgive others for their wrongdoings toward you, echoing the words of Ephesians 4:32: *And be ye kind to one another, tenderhearted, forgiving one another, even as God for Christ's sake hath forgiven you.* (KJV)

5. Pray against temptations

Let's face it: life has temptations. Just because we are Christian does not mean that every temptation of life magically goes away so we can be more comfortable. Second to want, I believe the most commonly prayed prayers are not for endurance and strength against temptation, but to be removed from difficulties and challenges. Many prayers people pray go something like the following: "Lord, please make so-and-so do what I want" or "God, do what I want!" Prayer is not like that at all; we don't pray so God can fix everyone else. It's definitely fine to pray for others or to ask God to intervene in someone's life, but it isn't right for us to be demanding in prayer that God conform to our will so we can be comfortable. A basic reality of life is that things will not always go our way, nor will we always like life's outcomes. People and circumstances both will prove trying, tempting, and difficult. We will find ourselves faced with choices and opportunities to slip up in our Christian walk through behavior, speech, or conduct. What should we do? Pray even before temptation comes upon us! James 1:2-3 reminds us: *My brethren, count it all joy when ye fall into divers temptations; Knowing this, that the trying of your faith worketh patience.* (KJV) This heralds the words of Soren Kierkegaard, "Prayer does not change God, it changes him who prays." We shouldn't be praying for specific material things all the time, but to grow in grace instead. We grow when we resist temptation and gain a great victory when we use prayer as a weapon against temptation.

> **AUTHOR'S REFLECTIONS**
>
> Prayer is our personal communication with God. If we aren't praying regularly, we aren't communicating with God as we should. When praying, voice what you need to say to God, but don't forget to listen! Divine communication does go two ways!

6. Pray for all that belongs to God

We know the Kingdom, the power, and the glory belong to God from reading the Scriptures. Do we remember to pray for all that belongs to God, and that we can reflect all that belongs to God?

Luke 17:21 tells us: *Nor will people say, Look! Here [it is]! or, See, [it is] there! For behold, the kingdom of God is within you [in your hearts] and among you [surrounding you].* (AMPC) We are a part of all that belongs to God! In our lives we should therefore act like we belong to God.

In praying for all that belongs to God, we too pray for ourselves, to receive the strength to live for the Kingdom every day and in every way. As representatives who belong to God, let's pray with a fervency that we can walk through the day bringing glory to the power and grace of His Kingdom. Such intent in prayers also reminds us to pray for all those who live and work in God's Kingdom and to support our brothers and sisters in Christ through edification.

Should we pray the "Our Father?"

There is nothing wrong with praying the Our Father, using Jesus' very words. For that matter, there is nothing wrong with praying any of Scripture's prayers. Throughout the Scriptures we find many records of individuals who prayed and heard from God. We should remember, however, that while there's nothing wrong praying in Jesus' words, Jesus was outlining a guide for us as to how to pray and what to pray for. None of the Bible's prayers were intended to become legalistic wordings and codes for religious gatherings. No matter what words we use in prayer, we must be sure to always pray with the right heart.

Should we take a certain posture in prayer?

The Bible lists many prayer postures: kneeling, standing, sitting, prostrate, looking up, and sitting, to name a few. There is no one posture that is more correct than another when it comes to prayer as long as our heart is in posture for prayer.

Be edified in prayer

Just as communication with other people can prove to build us up, so too does prayer edify us in our relationship with God. Prayer does not serve to be a religious chore we perform to make others around us happy. It is clear that living to pray in public and for display is wrong. Our prayer lives are not meant to be a weapon by which we attempt to get God to do what we want Him to do. Our prayer life is meant to be a refresher and edifier of everything good, noble, and spiritual. Through prayer, we tie our physical lives and realities to our spiritual lives and realities. The spiritual realm isn't beyond our reach; it is as near and as close to us as our next prayer. God isn't quite as distant as many proclaim Him to be, and what a gift prayer is to us that we can communicate and talk to God at any time: in good seasons and in bad, in times of plenty and lean times, and in praise and cries for help. No matter what we are doing or where we are, we can always communicate with God via the means of prayer. 1 Thessalonians 5:17 tells us to *Pray without ceasing.* How can this be accomplished? We must always remember that in everything we do, we are communicating with God through prayer, praise, obedience, and action. Prayer is a dutiful part of every aspect to every Christian's life, visible in so many ways. Make the commitment to make every moment of your life a prayer to God, your heavenly Father!

Apostle Marino preaching in Burlington, North Carolina (January 2015)

6 THE POWER OF SUGGESTION
(Volume 12, Number 3 – May/June 2014)

I recently had an encounter with a leader who claimed to be very enamored with my ministry and have great respect for me. I didn't know her very well, but something about her left me feeling uncomfortable. We'd only spoken a few times, but the few times we had, there was just something about her that made me very leery. Despite this fact, when she invited me to speak for her at an event, I initially accepted the invitation. We had a conversation on the phone that seemed positive, and I decided to put aside any misgivings I might have had about her. That ended when I received an inbox online from her the following day, telling me that I should leave my ministry and absorb into hers.

She's not the first to suggest this, but the way it was done was particularly sinister. She outright stated that doing so would be the way to get the "curse" off my ministry that she believed was present there. The way in which I was approached was both out of order and offensive. When I confronted her about it, she attacked me further, criticizing how I addressed the matter with her and that I misunderstood, thus she should have a right to explain. What was there to explain? Simply put, nothing. She delivered a word that she claimed was from God but was actually her speaking out of the flesh.

This might seem like a very obvious - and extreme - example. Most reading this can see how out of line and out of the flesh such a word was.

The thing that is not always so obvious, however, is the way in which people say, do, and tell us things every day out of the flesh, but pass them off as being a word of God to your life.

How can we tell what is God from what is not? With so many eager to provide a word, tell us something they feel is from God, or provide some insight into something for us - how do we know when we are receiving a word that is from God, or is not? How can we discern when God is speaking from what is someone's opinion - or suggestion - and what do we do with that?

Here a word, there a word...

Most people today want to feel a touch - or presence - of God in their lives on a personal level. In days gone by, our ancestors didn't seek out direct, personal word like we do today. When they had a personal need, they would pray and seek God for His guidance. They would look for a sign or some sort of revelation that would help them decide what to do. Even though the purpose might be the same, the means by which the purpose was accomplished was quite different. People were not as dependent on the thoughts and words of others to guide them into their decisions; they relied more on what they believed to be direct revelation from God. Instead of seeking out people, they would go to the throne first and seek personal guidance second.

Now we perceive God's presence differently. In a world full of technology, it is easier than ever to keep in contact with others, but it is not easier to be in contact. People long for a personal touch, something that lets them know they've heard from God in a more visible and tangible way. The way this is often done today is through the form of what we call a "word," most usually a reference to a word of wisdom or a word of knowledge. Someone gives someone else this word based on their situation, knowingly or unknowingly. Oftentimes it is a very personal word, specific to a certain issue or situation someone is facing. Rather than

> **BEHIND THE ARTICLE**
>
> When I wrote this article, I was embroiled in a battle with several rebellious and unrelenting people who I had trained and covered, right at the same time as I had someone trying to indicate I should leave my ministry behind and join hers. All of what was going on related to "revelations" that others felt they received that were, in reality, false (i.e., not from God). It was a trying time, and as a result, I wanted to learn more about what God had to say about spiritual gifts such as word of knowledge and word of wisdom. The result was this article, which revealed clearly and with truth that following every spirit and every wind of teaching that comes our way – no matter how pretty it may come in a package – is a dangerous thing.

serving as guidance, it is considered to be a direct, literal revelatory word of God to the receiving individual through the person who gives this word.

Given word of knowledge and word of wisdom were not things commonly talked about in decades past, it is amazing the way receiving and giving "a word" has become the literal "it" thing in Christianity today. People seek out word, give words unsolicited, and request you to get a "word" for them, whether you have that gift or not. But what exactly are a word of knowledge and a word of wisdom? Are we understanding - and exercising these gifts properly?

Word of wisdom and word of knowledge

1 Corinthians 12:8 says the following: *To one is given in and through the [Holy] Spirit [the power to speak] a message of wisdom, and to another [the power to express] a word of knowledge and understanding according to the same [Holy] Spirit.* (AMPC) This tells us having the ability to give a word of knowledge or a word of wisdom is a gift from God. They are part of prophetic gifts, not necessarily indicating one is a prophet, but that one does hear from and know of the things of God. We also can tell given these are a part of the charismatic gifts, that anyone who is truly in God can, at any time, exercise this gift as God gives the grace and ability to do so.

Both a word of knowledge and a word of wisdom have a few things in common: both are given by God, both directly relate to a circumstance someone is in or something about their lives, and both directly give an instruction. They differ in that a word of knowledge provides information - it calls the issue out - and a word of wisdom gives specific directions to handle a situation or obedience. Both require the obedience of the hearer - they must attend to whatever has been instructed and they must act accordingly.

The major thing we need to consider when it comes to giving or receiving a 'word" is the ability to hear - and discern - spirits. There are many people who do hear from a spirit in this world, but that does not mean they are hearing from the Spirit of God. It is essential that if we are going to walk in a gift of word of knowledge or word of wisdom or we are

---

KEY VERSE: 1 JOHN 4:1-3

Beloved, do not believe every spirit, but test the spirits to see whether they are from God, for many false prophets have gone out into the world. By this you know the Spirit of God: every spirit that confesses that Jesus Christ has come in the flesh is from God, and every spirit that does not confess Jesus is not from God. This is the spirit of the antichrist, which you heard was coming and now is in the world already. (ESV)

going to seek such out - that we also ask for discernment on every matter.

Test every spirit

In 1 John 4:1-6, the Apostle John issues the most practical - and purposed - advice when it comes to spiritual matters: *Beloved, do not believe every spirit, but test the spirits to see whether they are from God, for many false prophets have gone out into the world. By this you know the Spirit of God: every spirit that confesses that Jesus Christ has come in the flesh is from God, and every spirit that does not confess Jesus is not from God. This is the spirit of the antichrist, which you heard was coming and now is in the world already. Little children, you are from God and have overcome them, for he who is in you is greater than he who is in the world. They are from the world; therefore they speak from the world, and the world listens to them. We are from God. Whoever knows God listens to us; whoever is not from God does not listen to us. By this we know the Spirit of truth and the spirit of error.* (ESV) It's very obvious that spirits go forth in the world and that they deceive people. We can hear, abide by, and embrace all sorts of things received from the paranormal realm. Well-intentioned, nice, even seemingly spiritual people can receive words and be under the power of influences that are not of God.

We live in a church largely dominated by emotions, feelings, and opinions. People are much more easily swayed by various forces and influences than we might like to imagine, simply because they have certain wants and desires that leave them open to suggestions. It is why we must assess spirits by the requirements listed above: someone who is giving you a direct word into your life needs to recognize Jesus Christ as Lord at the time they are giving you that word; they need to not be someone who is against the anointing nor presence of God present in this world, and on someone's life; and they need to be able to separate themselves in the flesh from the word they receive to bring forth in the Spirit. When we are objective about the words we are delivering, we are less likely to deliver something counterfeit than if we are caught up in emotion or speaking something over someone else that reflects something we may want, hope, or think for them.

Giving a "word" to someone is not just a matter of speaking random things or using the means of knowledge or wisdom to try and express our situations about someone else's situation. It's not a time to use the things of God to be messy or to be up in other people's business. It is also not an avenue to gossip or try and get people to give details about personal information.

The test of a prophet

Joseph Smith. Herbert Armstrong. Brigham Young. Pat Robertson. All the men listed here meet the Biblical definition of "false prophets." There are many more people out there throughout history and in this world today who claim to be able to speak for God, the words of God, and the thoughts of God, who, are, actually false prophets. It may seem harsh or judgmental to label someone a false prophet, but God desires that we protect ourselves against those who speak false words in His Name. In Deuteronomy 18:18-22, we learn how to distinguish true prophets from false ones: *I will raise them up a Prophet from among their brethren, like unto thee, and will put my words in his mouth; and he shall speak unto them all that I shall command him. And it shall come to pass, that whosoever will not hearken unto My words which he shall speak in My Name, I will require it of him. But the prophet, which shall presume to speak a word in My Name, which I have not commanded him to speak, or that shall speak in the name of other gods, even that prophet shall die. And if thou say in thine heart, How shall we know the word which the Lord hath not spoken? When a prophet speaketh in the name of the Lord, if the thing follow not, nor come to pass, that is the thing which the Lord hath not spoken, but the prophet hath spoken it presumptuously: thou shalt not be afraid of him.* (KJV) In other words: if what somebody says materializes or comes to pass, that means they received the word God gave them. If it does not materialize or come to pass, the word was not genuinely from God.

As a word of knowledge and a word of wisdom are gifts that fall under the heading of the prophetic, we can apply the same litmus test to the words we receive from people. If someone is telling you they have received a 'word' for you, the word given needs to somehow apply, come true, or come to pass. If it doesn't, it is time to step back and test the spirit at work in the situation. If something is spoken that seems completely off, it's time to seriously seek God as to whether or not that word was from him. When a word is given to us that is a suggestion rather than true guidance from God, we do not need to fear rejecting it or not applying it to our lives.

Why we have a word of knowledge and a word of wisdom

It's important to remember the reason why God has given us the abundance of spiritual gifts we have in the church today. They do not exist to make us feel good, feel all warm and fuzzy, to have high self-esteem, or to impose our own viewpoints on others. The reason God has given us the word of knowledge and word of wisdom is to edify the Body of Christ, the church. God knew that there would be situations arising in the lives of believers and matters arising in the history of the church that would require guidance, inspiration, knowledge, and wisdom as each situation arose. This means the word of knowledge and word of wisdom have specific applications for us within the guidance and bounds of what is true or what is false. The word of knowledge and word of wisdom do not exist so that we can have our decisions and choices made for us.

As believers, we need to establish some healthy boundaries when it comes to accepting every single "word" someone gives to us. Yes, there are many people who genuinely have these gifts and who exercise them with accuracy and purpose. There are then those who may have a genuine gift but have not been trained or taught how to use it wisely or with purpose. Sometimes people give a word that may be accurate, but as they do not have the discernment to recognize the times, they are speaking that word out of season or out of turn. There are times when someone may speak something that is not yet to be spoken. For all these reasons, we need to make it very clear within ourselves what we will do when suggestions arise in contrast and opposition to what we know God has already revealed to us.

> **AUTHOR'S REFLECTIONS**
>
> We should never, ever be people who are so eager for a word that we start seeking one out anywhere and everywhere. Being a Christian means having faith, and sometimes faith means not getting the sign we want, the word we want, or the feeling that we desire to glean from our situation. In these "silent periods," we are still called to trust God and move forward.

Run to the throne, not the phone

The reason we have such a rise in false prophets and falsified guidance today is because we are so eager to feel like we have some sort of personal touch or approval, we are forsaking common sense and seeking God before we seek out someone else for word or guidance on a matter. It's natural to want confirmation, comfort, even to recognize the presence of God in a true word of God and a true confirmation. We can, however, reach a point where we have grown so dependent upon that point of contact with others that we run to other people before we seek out the direction of God. In this type of climate, we open ourselves up for spirits that need extensive testing. It is great to receive a word, it is great to receive confirmation, I will even go as far as to say that it can really bring a great sense of God's presence when God is truly in it. We cannot, however, substitute running to people for running to God. Many of the matters we take to God, hoping to receive a word about, are not things that require such extensive guidance or confirmation. Sometimes we just don't want to deal with something or accept what we are going through, and we want someone else to validate how we are feeling about whatever that issue or thing may be.

We also need to learn to stand on God's promises and words to us in a greater way. We should not be so weak in our faith that we go seeking people out to tell us, once again, what God has already told us. It's great to receive confirmation, but when God speaks to us (and we know it is God we have heard from), we should have the faith - and the resolve - to trust in what we have heard, whether someone tells us it's right, or approves of it, or not.

Hebrews 11:1 gives us some important backing about the realities of faith: *Now faith is the substance of things hoped for, the evidence of things not seen.* (KJV) We quote this verse frequently, but do we consider what it is saying? Hebrews 11:1 is telling us that faith is the substance, or the stuff, of the things that are hoped (promised, not yet received) for, and is the evidence, or proof, of things that have not been seen or materialized. This means that faith is something that proves itself. We have faith when we stand up and realize we don't yet have or walk fully in what God has for us or has promised to us. A word of knowledge and a word of wisdom are designed to help us on this faith journey. They exist so we can continue to believe and continue to be encouraged as we progress toward all we hope for. They don't exist to derail us, cause us doubt or unbelief, or substitute anything for true faith in our experiences and situations.

In this day and age, we need to surround ourselves with people who genuinely walk in gifts and use their gifts for the glory of God rather than the power of suggestion. If you feel bullied by a word, misled by one, or just confused - seek out God's ministry of discernment. Talk to Him yourself, seek out a trusted person who can help with guidance, and most of all, trust in the ways of God and faith to lead you rather than being misled and misguided by people - no matter how well-intentioned someone may be.

Apostle Marino ministering in Durham, North Carolina (February 2013)

7 THE CENTER OF HIS WILL
(Volume 13, Number 1—First Quarter 2015)

The "will" of God. Finding the will of God for our lives. Discerning God's will for us. Even though we don't necessarily hear much on these topics on a regular basis, discussions about the will of God are most popular, especially among new Christians. I remember talking to a woman many years ago about the issue of healing and God's will in her life. Even though she knew she was out of God's will, and fully well knew what God's will for her was, she did not want to align with God's will. Knowingly she disobeyed and still wanted God's deliverance without obedience. Needless to say, she was never healed; yet it was beyond her why she never received the physical redemption she sought. It was a sorry state to see a woman so clearly out of the will of God fail to understand that alignment with God is essential to one who knows of Him, especially when it comes to matters of healing.

Throughout both the Old and New Testaments we find repeated emphasis on the will of God: discovering what it is, obeying it, and remaining in it. God's Word could not be clearer: our basic command as believers is to make the proclamation found in John 3:30: *He must increase, but I must decrease. [He must grow more prominent; I must grow less so.]* (AMPC) The basic command to center ourselves fully in God's will means we must decrease ourselves - our own personal selfishness, control issues, wants, and desires - and come to a place where we align what we've always sought for ourselves with what God seeks for us. It is essential for anyone who calls themselves a Christian to grab hold of this revelation and begin to pursue life in the center of God's will.

For a topic that is so highly emphasized, highlighted, underlined, and bolded throughout Scripture, we seldom if ever hear about the will of God once we are beyond the basics of being a believer. It is naturally assumed that every Christian, no matter what they are doing in their lives, is simply in God's will - and this body continues to mount in favor of people who have no idea about God's will; they simply think anything goes, anything they do is acceptable, and that they have a free ticket to heaven, so nothing else matters.

It is obvious that discerning the will of God and living in God's will is a very important aspect to being one who claims to believe in God, trust in Him, and follow His will. We know it is relevant in order to lead a life full of witness, blessing, and promise from God. But does the will of God relate to other aspects of our life, our faith, and the outcome of situations we find ourselves in?

> **BEHIND THE ARTICLE**
>
> Discovering the will of God has always been a very popular topic within our ministry teaching and discussions. This article was the result of a request I had as pertains to discovering the will of God deeper in someone's life. This particular article ran three times in *Power For Today* Magazine over six years due to its enduring popularity, and this is the last – and longest – version of that teaching.

The devil, the devil, the devil!

It's not uncommon to find Christians who talk more about the devil than they do about God. There are two reasons for this. The first reason is because they believe the devil is the cause of every problem they have in their life and everything that seems to go wrong in their circumstances. Any time an individual doesn't get what they think they want, they blame it on the devil. The second reason is because of this type of teaching, Christians have failed to see the relationship between choice and results. In other words, Christians don't understand the basic way that Satan (or God, for that matter), operates.

We can recognize from the Word the way Satan operates is through people's choices. Through sinful behaviors, attitudes, disobedience to God, rebellion, evildoing, or other wrongdoing, we conform our will to the will of Satan. The reality is that while some attacks from the enemy are certainly unprecedented and come with the purpose to derail us from our righteous course - take Job, for example - often the circumstances by which Satan takes hold in a believer's life are due to the choices of the individual which are out of step with God's will. James 4:7 gives us proof that it is when we follow the will of God that the devil does not gain foothold in our lives: *Submit yourselves, then, to God. Resist the devil, and he will flee from you.* Satan gains ground in our lives when we give him that ground through our cooperation, either direct or indirect, with his plans rather than the plans of God. In other words, Satan gains ground through each one of us - and the whims, actions, thoughts, and emotions we surrender to his purposes.

As a counterfeit, Satan has inversely used God's method of choice for evil. Living in the will of God, however, operates in the same way as living in the will of Satan: it is by our choice. Through our choices, actions, and behaviors, we choose to do the will of God. God doesn't force anyone to be saved. He doesn't force anyone to choose His ways or to obey His will. While it is His great hope that all will come to great knowledge of His will and obey it, God's system mandates we do so by our free choice. 1 Thessalonians 4:3-8 enlightens us to the behavior of an individual who aspires to walk fully in the will of God: *It is God's will that you should be sanctified: that you should avoid sexual immorality; that each of you should learn to control his own body in a way that is holy and honorable, not in passionate lust like the heathen, who do not know God; and that in this matter no one should wrong his brother or take advantage of him. For God did not call us to be impure, but to live a holy life. Therefore, he who rejects this instruction does not reject man but God, Who gives you His Holy Spirit.* This passage clearly makes it evident that our choice to live in God's will is manifest by our conduct. We can't be people who say we believe in God and want to do His will and then never act like it. It also shows that living in the will of God is far deeper than just picking out a career path or deciding how to spend one's life. If we truly want to eliminate the devil from our lives we have to consistently make the effort not to follow the ways of passions - which are far more encompassing than just in a sexual sense, but speak of deep, persistent desire in one's life - and instead replace our own personal wants, wills, and weaknesses with the will of God. It is something we do on purpose!

KEY VERSE: JOHN 3:30

He must increase, but I must decrease. [He must grow more prominent; I must grow less so.] (AMPC)

"But I don't wanna!!!"

One of the most consistent reasons why people fail to walk in the will of God is because they break each situation down into circumstances and assess what God calls them to by whether or not they want to do what God is asking of them. Today we put a lot of emphasis on feelings, thoughts, and yes, desires for a situation. If we don't feel that we want to do something or think that something isn't going to benefit us in an obvious way, we assume God isn't in it or they assume the devil is somehow working against us. Too much of what we desire to do or seek to do often comes down to nothing more than whether or not we want to do it, thus making the will of God seem changeable and selfish. With an almost whimsical approach to understanding God's will, it seems like God's will can vary at any moment.

Such a breakdown may be common, but it also brings great distortion to understanding the precept of living in the center of God's will. It is true that following God's will does mean there will be times when He asks something of us that we would rather not do. But living and doing the will of God is far deeper than just doing things we don't like. When we live in the will of God, we find ourselves aligned with Him in both a spiritual or practical sense. It is not about us and what we want or do not want anymore but instead about what God wants and trusting that His will is ultimately what will lead us to wholeness. Philippians 2:12-14 gives the following advice: *Therefore, my dear friends, as you have always obeyed—not only in my presence, but now much more in my absence—continue to work out your salvation with fear and trembling, for it is God Who works in you to will and to act according to His good purpose. Do everything without complaining or arguing...* Walking in the will of God is about that process of salvation, that working towards perfection possible even this side of heaven. As we work toward that ultimate goal, our will purposes more for His - and we walk toward the fully good purpose of God, without grumbling, complaining, or arguing.

Not my will...

One of the hardest things to develop within the Christian walk is discerning our will from God's will. In today's church, it's amazing how much people pass off their own will as the will of God simply because they have never developed the strong precept of spiritual discernment. One of the first ways we develop that discernment is through a process known as detachment. When we detach ourselves from a circumstance, it means that we step back and remove our own personal opinions, biases, and thoughts from it and simply look at it as it is objectively. Often taking the time to detach from a situation brings clarity to God's will within it as He directs us to the answer we seek. We can't be so caught up in our feelings, emotions, and concepts all the time that we keep missing the will of God in our situations and that we make our judgments and calls based on things that can change and fade as quickly as they rise and cause us to feel a certain way.

The second step is to distinguish God's direction from personal want. It's real easy to brush passages like: *Whoever does God's will is My brother and sister and mother.* (Mark 3:35) without a thought to what it is really saying; but we must recognize that individuals who genuinely do the will of God enjoy a relationship with the Father and with Christ Himself that those who pursue their own will never have because they have learned how to distinguish what is God from what is them. It's not just people who are believers who become the brothers and sisters of Christ, it is those who come to do God's will because Jesus did God's will.

These two basic steps combined launch into the third and final phase of following God's will: obedience. We talk far more in church about what God should do for us than what we should do for Him, and the result is a selfish church. We do for God through our unconditional obedience to Him, even if it winds us up in a less-than desirable situation. Remember, Jesus' obedience to the Father rendered Him the cross - but the resurrection was not that far behind!

Validating our message

Christians love the idea of a world converted to Christ. There is something about the concept that gets any on-fire Christian excited at the hint of its possibility. As nice of a concept as it is, the reality is that our message will not find its realization without our validation. How can Christians expect others to want to follow God if they aren't doing it themselves? It's great to talk about the blessings of God, the goodness of God, the power of God, and the ability of God to transform lives; but the reality behind all that is the truth that every one of those aspects of our relationship with God is conditional upon our obedience to Him and our step with His will.

In John 17:17, Jesus gives us a powerful word on this topic: *If anyone chooses to do God's will, he will find out whether My teaching comes from God or whether I speak on My own.* (NIV) The reason people could discern whether or not Jesus' teachings were true by following God's will is because He was following God's will. The same is true for us: if what we teach, proclaim, or do is within the will of God, others will recognize it for truth as they too imitate following the will of God in their lives.

If we want to be good representatives of the Gospel - leaders of truth among others in our lives - we need to be good disciples of God's will. Do you want to be a better representative of God in your life? Be a better disciple of His will and stop making your own voice the one you obey when it comes to essential matters of purpose and faith in life.

Our ways are not His ways

> **AUTHOR'S REFLECTIONS**
>
> Being in the center of God's will may seem challenging because it requires us to truly seek Him in a way that many are unwilling to do so. Being out of His will, however, is much harder!

Another reason why it can be so difficult to discern the will of God is because the ways of God are not our ways. What may make sense to us and may seem good, doable, or purposeful to us may be the exact opposite of what God asks us to do. It can be hard to reconcile this conflict within oneself, especially when you can't figure out what God has in store or in plan for you. When it comes to these situations, we have to put ourselves aside; let go of the control and the attitude that we know what is best; and stop trying so hard to figure things like this out all the time. Following the will of God is a sign of our level of trust in Him. While many may like to sing pretty songs about trusting in God and following Him, it's a lot more relevant to actually live in that trust and follow God, even when it's hard.

Our faith is tested most when confronted with a situation we just don't understand, and yet trust God for it, anyway. We can trust that God will not bring us to shame, just as we recognize the Gospel will not bring us to shame. In Romans 1:16-17, Paul raises a point often quoted by Christians yet seldom understood: *I am not ashamed of the gospel, because it is the power of God for the salvation of everyone who believes: first for the Jew, then for the Gentile. For in the gospel a righteousness from God is revealed, a righteousness that is by faith from first to last, just as it is written: 'The righteous will live by faith.'* (NIV) Living by faith means we make a deliberate effort to follow the will of God, even when we don't understand everything about it. Faith means we don't have to understand everything; we just have to trust in God.

By living in faith, we already have our answer and know the hope of every promise shall be realized as we remain in God's full will for us at all times.

A deliberate, on purpose walk with God

As I studied Scripture for this article, I was amazed to see how many passages in the Bible related to will, both God's and ours. Repeatedly the Bible states that God willed something either instantaneous or prophetic, and it was done. This tells us that much of what happens throughout salvation history and in our personal relationships with Him happens deliberately and on purpose because it is what God has commanded. The same is true when we look at things on our end - we are to will our will to His - deliberately, on purpose, and with effort. Following the will of God doesn't just jump on us one day and overtake us. We must pursue it and make that effort every day, in every situation that rises up, with every question that comes along, to follow what God has for us.

Matthew 7:13-14 says: *Enter through the narrow gate. For wide is the gate and broad is the road that leads to destruction, and many enter through it. But small is the gate and narrow the road that leads to life, and only a few find it.* A hard, undeniable truth about the Christian life is that it is not an easy walk. The world doesn't understand it, we often can't comprehend what God is doing through or in us, and it is a constant, deliberate action to die to self every day and say "yes" to God instead. No wonder only a few find it! If being a serious, dedicated Christian took no effort at all, the entire world would be saved by now.

As we go along in the Christian life, we experience the pressure of that narrow road: as the road narrows, it increases the pressure upon us to change, grow, and develop into the image of God in a deeper sense than mere creation, but rather, a new creation. Living in the will of God means it's not all about us. We deal with the realization that God may have things in store for us and through us that have nothing to do with our own personal comfort, security, or feeling good. While we trust and know God always has us in His hands, we must trust it is there even when we can't see it in our natural eyes. In following the will of God, we find the road which leads to life. So many people today live lives that aren't really lived - they just get up, do their thing, and go to bed, not experiencing purpose, meaning, or significance in their existence. The option between living a purposeless existence and living life is summed up in one thing: the will of God. As we grow in our understanding of choosing God's will, we can see it is the bottom line to the ultimate purpose in this life and the next.

Discovering the will of God is an unfolding journey, but it is not a process that requires one to undertake strange practices or many hours of meditation. We don't come to a better understanding of God by being super-spiritual or avoiding life. Walking in God's will is not achieved by trying to live in any other way than that which He calls us to live. Because we know that the road God has us on is one that leads to life, the answer to the will of God comes from walking in and living life. That means in our everyday lives, we can achieve a deeper understanding of what it means to be in His will. As we do both supernatural and simple things, we can see the will of God manifest more clearly for us. The obvious ways in which God works for us in our lives, the subtle ways He intervenes on our behalf when things are difficult or tricky, all relate to a deep and profound understanding of the way in which God moves on our behalf because His will represents a perfection for us.

Dedication to the will of God

It's a sobering fact when we realize that if it weren't for God, we would be nowhere in our lives. It is only within the will of God that we make it out of Egypt and work toward the Promised Land, even if that journey takes many years. If we will only get serious about pursuing the will of God, we can trust that we will gain greater insight into God's purpose for us in every area and see in a deeper way why He places us in the circumstances and surrounding that He does. Sometimes we are in our atmospheres to make a difference in someone else's life, and sometimes our atmosphere is supposed to give us a greater understanding or deeper perspective for our own lives. It can also help us to understand the power of our choices: that it may very well not be the devil, but our own choice to cooperate with him, that takes us away from God. Finding the center of His will gives us a greater awe and respect for the Creator of the Universe, the Savior of mankind, and the Father of us all, Who cares enough about us to give us a life fully centered in Him.

8 DISCERNING DISCERNMENT
(Volume 10, Number 10 – October 2011)

On the way to my Arabic class a few months ago, the Lord spoke something to me in the car: "Discernment is the gift of 'knowing better.'" I loved it when God spoke it to me, and I love it now. In one simple statement, the Lord summarized the essence of the gift of discernment: it is "knowing better." Discernment is a gift of knowledge and wisdom. It is, in its essence, the gift of knowing and knowing the truth behind what may appear, what may seem to be, or what may look a certain way. The bottom line of discernment: it is a ministry of truth (Psalm 119:125, Proverbs 3:21, Proverbs 17:10, Proverbs 28:11).

For many years I walked in the gift of discernment, and I didn't realize what it was: I just called it "a knowing." I would be sitting in a situation where everything spoke one thing, and I would just have this gnawing knowing deep down within that told me something else. About two years ago I sat in a McDonald's in Puerto Rico with my former apostle and four other women. I was there for her conference and the conference itself went fine. The women present were responsive and interested, and it was universal that they wanted me back the following year. Everyone at that table, my former leader included, told me I would be back next year...yet I sat there...and inside I had this knowing feeling that I wouldn't be back. I knew I wasn't returning. Nothing in my circumstances spoke to me that I wouldn't be back. Everything looked great and promising, the encouragement that things were good was evident, and there was nothing to indicate otherwise. But...I knew. Six months later, I was no longer under my former leader and there was no chance I was going back for her event. In that specific instance, discernment let me know what circumstances were not - and discernment was right.

We don't hear much about discernment in today's church. We like to hear a lot about healing, about tongues, about faith, and about ministering...but we don't like to talk about discernment. I think the reason we avoid discernment is because somewhere inside of many in the church today there is the avoidance of 'knowing better.' In a discerning church, we know better than to think prophets walk in a building and start speaking cars, money, and houses over a church in total disrepair and totally out of order. We would know better than to just believe what someone says as truth because they are on TV or the radio. We wouldn't just throng to every leader and teacher who seems to have a name that is visible to the public. What we would do is rightly assess every teaching, every leader, and every circumstance according to the Holy Spirit.

> **BEHIND THE ARTICLE**
>
> Discernment has always been a gift that I heavily walk in. So much so, in fact, that it has often caused me to be very uncomfortable in different settings because I was able to so effectively discern and pick up on the spirits present in people and situations. Uncomfortable or not, I truly believe that discernment has gotten me out of some difficult – and possibly dangerous – situations throughout my walk in ministry.

A ministry of the Holy Spirit

Discernment is, first and foremost, a ministry of the Holy Spirit. We learn in John 14:26: *But the Counselor, the Holy Spirit, whom the Father will send in My Name, will teach you all things and will remind you of everything I have said to you.* If the Holy Spirit guides us into all truth, that means that, by the Holy Spirit, we are able to discern what is true from what is false. It's not some sort of spooky, ethereal thing, but something practical in everyday life. As the Holy Spirit inspires the Word, we recognize the truth of the Holy Spirit in the interpretation, guidance, and reading of the Word. It also means that we know what is true by the Word. The ministry of discernment is what makes the ministry of the Holy Spirit alive and active in our lives. When we are in situations that raise questions, it is the Spirit that brings the Word of Truth to our recall and our hearts (John 17:17, 1 Corinthians 2:13).

Right here we've said a mouthful that we need to consider deeper. The ministry of discernment is, indeed, about discerning truth in every situation. It also tells us about error, which is the opposite of truth. In being able to identify truth, we are also able to identify error. Through discernment, we have the ability to discern all types of error: those pertaining to doctrine, those pertaining to our spiritual lives, and those pertaining to our everyday lives...because they are all connected. In the Bible, it says that Jesus knew the thoughts of the Pharisees and leaders (Matthew 12:25). This wasn't telepathy, this was discernment! As the Way, the Truth, and the Life (John 14:6), discernment was a practical part of His everyday life and interaction. It wasn't just about doctrine, it was about knowing who walked among Him, who was for Him, and who was against Him. When we walk in discernment, we can operate the same type of gift, knowing who is for us, who is against us, and who to trust and who not to trust.

Clarifying spiritual confusion

Spiritual things can sound complicated when they are explained. Sometimes I think people do this on purpose, to make themselves sound smarter or more enlightened than others. Sometimes I just think it happens because the individual trying to present the issue tries to encompass too wide a scope and doesn't break the matter down enough for us...in other words, they don't operate in a lot of discernment. Discernment helps to break down some of these complicated spiritual things and make them practical. For this reason, discernment is awesome because it makes it so we don't have to question so much all the time: God gives us the ability simply to "know" as needed. With discernment, we don't have to memorize the whole Bible, we don't have to carry around a Bible commentary, or constantly text or message people for interpretation. When matters arise, issues arise, spirits arise, problems arise...God gives us the ability to know.

Discernment operates in a few different areas. Some of them we are familiar with, some we are not, and some we hear a lot about, but we do not have understanding about them.

Discerning of spirits

The most common area we hear discernment mentioned is in the area of discerning spirits (1 Corinthians 12:10). Applying discernment as a gift of "knowing better," discernment allows an individual the ability to know when

> **KEY VERSE: MATTHEW 12:25**
>
> Jesus knew their thoughts.

a spirit is of God or is not of God. This is a broad category of discernment: it applies to the words people speak over us, prophetic revelation claimed to be from God, the interactions of a person who claims to be of God, and the spirit that may need to be cast out of someone. Discerning of spirits also has a broader application: it is, simply put, discerning spirits. It is being able to identify what a spirit is, from the Holy Spirit to Jezebel. Discerning spirits helps the church remain clean; know what needs being cast out and when; and what type of spirit is present in what person, church, ministry, etc. It also helps to identify order and disorder. Discerning of spirits is, therefore, essential to all facets of ministry: apostolic, prophetic, evangelistic, pastoral, teaching, deliverance, healing, interpretation, and beyond. Every call, every facet of ministry can benefit from the ability to discern spirits. When we can identify a spirit, we can rightly assess how to handle or deal with that spirit.

Discerning true leaders from false ones

Jesus tells us: *Watch out that no one deceives you.* (Matthew 24:4) *See: I have told you ahead of time.* (Matthew 24:25) These words come right before and after prophecies about false leaders, people who will work miracles, and will be false christs, leaders, and messiahs to come. What does this tell us? Every one of us, from the greatest in the Kingdom to the least, has the ability to grow and walk in discernment. If we go against something we know, by discernment, to be true, we will have to be accountable for that. Discernment lets us know when a leader is false or true and we are called to stand on that discernment. With discernment, there is no excuse for following a false leader!

Practical wisdom on matters of revelation

Revelation is an awesome thing: I describe it as God "turning the light on." Revelation is a great power in the life of a believer, because it is a form of *rhema* word. What we must remember about revelation, however, is that *rhema* is not in contrast or contradiction to the *Logos*: they are a compliment, a part of a whole understanding of God's Word. Jesus Himself is the Logos, the ultimate revelation of revelation and Word together (John 1:1-14). That having been said...not every thought, feeling, opinion, or even lesson we may have from God can be classified as "revelation" and should not be taught as such because it misrepresents true revelation. Then we have the fact that there are different types of revelation. Some revelation just pertains to us as people. It may be something God gives us that will help us with a difficult situation, to help us grow as people, or to correct us about something - and it is so specific and personal to us, the revelation God is giving to us isn't meant to be shared with everybody else. There is revelation that is meant to be shared with everyone: be it a message, a teaching, a personal experience that, through revelation, God has shown us how to make it universal, or some sort of word for our day and age. Then there are areas of revelation that are meant to be shared at some time, just not right at the moment. Beyond these issues, we need to truly understand revelation from other things. If a so-called "revelation" somebody has is in contradiction to the Word, that sets a revelation in conflict with the *Logos* - and *rhema* and *Logos* cannot cancel each other out. Discernment is helpful to understand revelation, what you do with it, how it applies in a greater sense (if it does at all), and whether or not something is a revelation from God to begin with.

Knowing what is error, right, and wrong

Discernment is a practical gift, which means it applies in everyday situations. We tend to talk about discernment in terms of spirits, but discernment also applies to knowing when something is right or wrong to do as well as knowing when something is being done or said to us is right or wrong. Does someone just not seem right to you, but you can't explain it? Are you being lied to? Is someone working witchcraft around you? Are you besieged by the spirits of control and manipulation within your midst? Is someone praying for you and your benefit? Do you see God working for you in a situation? All of these "knowing senses" are discernment working practically in your life and helping you to "walk with God" on a daily basis (Genesis 5:22, Genesis 5:24, Genesis 6:9, Leviticus 26:13, Jeremiah 7:23).

Knowing when we were hearing from God and when we are not

It's easy to be swayed by the opinions of those around us. Sometimes the holiest people come and start telling us they have a "word from God" on our behalf and it's nothing more than their own undiscerning self, trying to dispense their opinions and advice. We must be careful about accepting the advice of others as the word of God because sometimes advice or opinions - no matter how good they may be, how well-intentioned it may seem, or how much we may like what they have to say - may mislead us from God's appointed purpose for us. We all want to hear we won't have to go through anything, suffer, deal with problems, encounter stress, and that our victory/breakthrough is nigh...which means that an awful lot of people feed our desire to hear that right back at us. Sometimes people tell us things and we know it's God...other times, somewhere inside, we know it's not God. That's discernment working within us to remain with God rather than hoping for something that isn't for us or out of His timing.

Knowing how to conduct ourselves

> **AUTHOR'S REFLECTIONS**
>
> When people ask me what spiritual gift or gifts they should pray to receive, discernment is always the first one I recommend. It's not the most showy of spiritual gifts and it certainly may not win popularity contests, but it makes work and ministry so much more effective in the long run.

I've heard people say they wish that God would just tell them how to behave in every situation. My answer: "Get some discernment and you'll know what to do in every situation!" We know the Word tells us in Ecclesiastes 3:1-8: *There is a time for everything, and a season for every activity under heaven: a time to be born and a time to die, a time to plant and a time to uproot, a time to kill and a time to heal, a time to tear down and a time to build, a time to weep and a time to laugh, a time to mourn and a time to dance, a time to scatter stones and a time to gather them, a time to embrace and a time to refrain, a time to search and a time to give up, a time to keep and a time to throw away, a time to tear and a time to mend, a time to be silent and a time to speak, a time to love and a time to hate, a time for war and a time for peace.* (NIV) It is by discernment that we learn when it is time to do what: be silent, speak, what to let live, what to kill, plant, uproot, heal, tear down, build, weep, laugh, mourn, dance, scatter, gather, embrace, refrain, search, give up, keep, throw away, tear, mend, love, hate, war, and peace. All of the things mentioned therein are a part of life; in fact, if we truly discern Ecclesiastes 3, it is giving us different phases of discernment throughout life that every single one of us will face. The Bible doesn't give us a road map of conduct in every single one of these situations, which means how we approach them is left up to our own discernment process as we walk with the Holy Spirit throughout life. Discernment proves that our walk with God is life-long; it is a process; and it doesn't begin and end because we end one phase of life or start another one.

Knowing how to witness to non-believers and the brethren

In today's church we aren't taught how to meet people's needs or even read them. What we are encouraged to do is "get out there and tell other people about Jesus!" This is an awesome command, and something I don't question...but are we doing it the right way? If we listen to discernment and just follow the fact that most people think Christians are obnoxious and annoying, we are missing something in our witness of our Lord to others. Jesus didn't "witness" the same way to everyone. Some people He talked to, some people He healed, some people He was very short with, with other people He was very compassionate and sensitive. Jesus' witness with the twelve disciples who became apostles was radically different than His witness to a blind man, to the woman caught in adultery, or to the Pharisees. Why? Because Jesus discerned a need for different interactions as a witness with these different people. Not everyone wants to hear the story of what God did for you in your life. Nobody wants to hear all the things you think are wrong with them because they aren't like you. Nobody likes a nag! Some people DO need to hear your story...just not right away. Some people just need a hug, some compassion, and an empathetic ear. Some people may have questions they need real answers to - not the answers you read in a tract in 1990. Discernment operates here as we walk in touch with the Spirit to recognize bringing people to know the Lord isn't a cosmic poker tournament, but about souls in need and reaching out to those people to see that God is real and He still meets needs, even today. The same is true in our support of other believers. We all operate in love, but the way I may need people to show me they love and care about me may be radically different than the way someone else needs to see love among other believers. As we walk in the Spirit, we can see ways we can encourage others, love others, bring others to the Lord, and stand stronger as the Body of Christ.

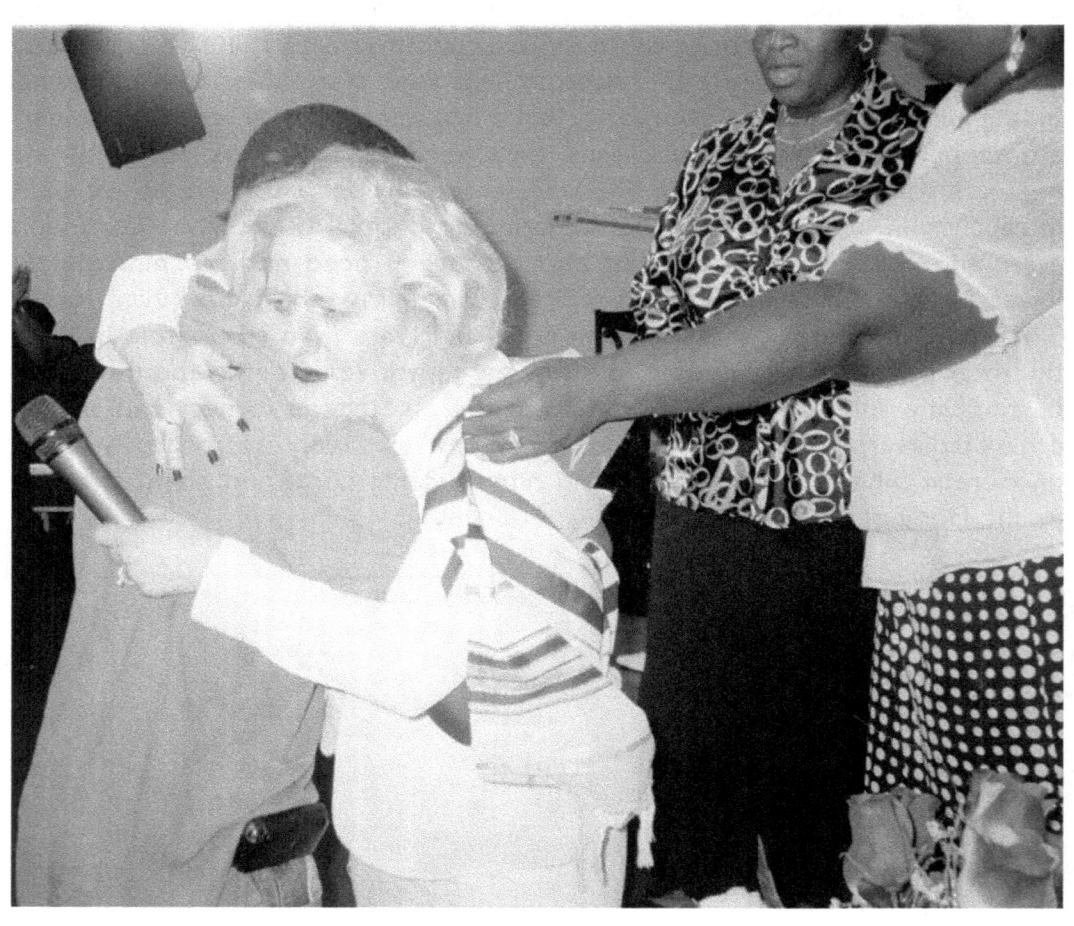

Apostle Marino ministering in Chesapeake, Virginia (September 2009)

9 CLASS ACTION
(Volume 10, Number 1 – January 2011)

As a Roman Catholic for seventeen years, I grew up hearing a lot about poverty. The Catholic Church was quick to expound the blessings of those who lived in the poorest and most dire of conditions. They told us that poverty was the most desirable of all lifestyles as God would bless it with treasures beyond money. The poor were encouraged to remain poor; to have more children than was possible, to afford to receive the great blessing of poverty; and to continue in the church's teachings so the poor could understand the value in their sufferings this side of eternal life.

The one thing they failed to teach us was that even though the church might believe the poor were blessed by God, the poor had absolutely no value to the church. As the poor were not abundant with finances, that meant they couldn't contribute as much to the church as the rich were able. This equated to less preferential treatment for the poor than the rich. I always remember being so confused because I would hear so much about the blessing for the poor, and yet the church treated my own family, who had a less than substantial income, very badly - when we were supposedly the ones who were blessed! I would constantly contrast the way we were treated with the way others in the church were treated. There were some who were pitied for their circumstances, some who were dependent on the church for their needs, and still others who seemed to be in our camp - the one where we weren't quite at the bottom of the barrel, but close enough to the bottom that the church did not hold us in very high regard. All of us, classified as "poor," had one thing in common: we were treated very badly.

Then there was the man who owned the funeral home. He wore white patent leather shoes, expensive gold jewelry, and fancy, expensive suits. When he came in the church, people paid attention to him. Anything that he wanted was his. The priest took special time to talk to him and consider whatever his wants were. Even though he wasn't very involved with church service in a church that thrived on volunteerism, it didn't seem to matter. He had a lot of money, and the church saw fit to treat him in a manner that showed the rest of us where the buck saw fit to stop.

When I became a Christian, I thought I had finally broken free of financial class distinctions. Not only was I wrong, I encountered several other "class" distinctions as well. Whites vs. blacks, men vs. women, poor vs. rich, women vs. women, and a host of other odds have caused me to believe that ministry is just junior high with Bibles. Too many claiming to be in the ministry still center in little cliques, make a habit of catering to the rich and ignoring the poor, and make judgments about people based on what they wear, how expensive their shoes are, and where they come from. Despite what any one of us may like to believe about the church, we still experience the sting of class distinction...and many of us have not resolved our own class distinctions to rise above differences and embrace the heart of the Gospel.

> **BEHIND THE ARTICLE**
>
> *Class Action* was born out of severe injustices I was seeing in churches as I lived and worked within the southern United States for the first time. I was appalled that people would segregate church and that when the matter was discussed, the universal response was, "It shouldn't be this way, but it is." They are right – it shouldn't be that way – and it is essential that we, as believers, make efforts to move toward unity and understanding when division is present.

Class distinctions in Scripture

Class distinctions are not new in religion. Hinduism, one of the world's oldest religions if not the oldest surviving today, has a complex system of class distinctions known as the caste system. Due to the caste system, it is very difficult if not impossible for an individual to ever elevate between classes in their lifetime. The poor stay poor, and the rich stay rich, and the poor are considered lowly servants to the rich all throughout their days. Egyptian, Roman, and Greek societies all employed the use of slaves and likewise used social distinctions by which members of society were free to socialize with one another. The early worlds were based on different prohibitions - religious which in turn became secular in nature - that defined how different groups of people interacted, lived, and worked in the same space (but often apart).

One of the biggest class distinctions in ancient times was between that of Jew and Gentile. Jews did not associate with Gentiles as they felt Gentiles were an inferior people in culture, beliefs, and in race. For this reason, hostility emerged between Jews and Gentiles, especially as Gentile nations often controlled Jewish states. We can see reflections of these hostilities between groups in the New Testament as Jew and Gentile strove to become one new man in Christ rather than divided in pieces. The arguments about circumcision, dietary guidelines, Sabbath and Jewish holiday observances, treatment of the Greek widows, and the like all reflect the intense friction existing between the two groups. These issues were compounded by universal contempt for the poor and needy and disagreements about how to handle such in the church.

Despite the differences of the early church, we see Jew and Gentile, male and female, young and old, and poor and rich come together in unity for the Lord and to build the Kingdom. They had differences which they knew God called them to put aside and move beyond. What did they know that today's church seems to have missed?

Class distinctions are against the work of Christ

One thing we learn in the New Testament is that Jesus died not just to crush religious law, but the hand of legalism: that which divides and conquers people into classes. Ephesians 2:15 tells us: *By abolishing in His [own crucified] flesh the enmity {caused by} the Law with its decrees and ordinances {which He annulled}; that He from the two might create in Himself one new man {one new quality of humanity out of the two}, so making peace.* (AMPC) Out of Jesus' sacrifice we find a lack of class distinctions; remaining instead is one new body, the Body of Christ. This vital understanding is essential to unity within the church because it is the very understanding of the work of Christ. Christ's work was one of reconciliation, and we often talk of Christ as our Mediator, Who came and

KEY VERSE: GALATIANS 3:28-39

There is neither Jew nor Greek, there is neither bond nor free, there is neither male nor female: for ye are all one in Christ Jesus. And if ye be Christ's, then are ye Abraham's seed, and heirs according to the promise. (KJV)

reconciled our relationship with the Father. But Christ's work of reconciliation was not just our relationship to the Father; He also reconciled us one to another. We have no right to stand upon the laws of men which divide humanity into classes when faced with the Son of God Who destroyed them on the cross.

The rich are no better than the poor

Have you ever attended a church that treated the rich differently than the poor? If you can relate with the story I told in the beginning of this article, would you be surprised to learn that such behavior is strongly denounced in the New Testament? James 2:1-9 gives a stern warning to those who show preferential treatment to people based on financial status: *My brethren, hold not the faith of our Lord Jesus Christ, the Lord of glory, with respect of persons. For if there come into your synagogue a man with a gold ring, in fine clothing, and there come in also a poor man in vile clothing; and ye have regard to him that weareth the fine clothing, and say, Sit thou here in a good place; and ye say to the poor man, Stand thou there, or sit under my footstool; Do ye not make distinctions among yourselves, and become judges with evil thoughts? Hearken, my beloved brethren; did not God choose them that are poor as to the world to be rich in faith, and heirs of the kingdom which He promised to them that love Him? But ye have dishonored the poor man. Do not the rich oppress you, and themselves drag you before the judgment-seats? Do not they blaspheme the honorable Name by which ye are called? Howbeit if ye fulfil the royal law, according to the scripture, Thou shalt love thy neighbor as thyself, ye do well: but if ye have respect of persons, ye commit sin, being convicted by the law as transgressors.* (ASV) This great passage gets to the heart of the issue on preferential treatment. As people called to be free in Christ, we are to uphold the reconciliation He has set forth for us. If we are not going to do that, and instead revert back to the ways of the world with their class systems, we subject ourselves to be judged according to the law rather than by grace.

The Gospel is available to all: rich and poor alike. There is no price of the Gospel; one must simply hear and believe to begin a life with Christ. Whenever we divide the church by income, we allow a powerful foothold for the love of money to come in and overwhelm the body of believers. Rich and poor alike need to hear and embrace the message of salvation, and people of every income group need to feel that they can come to church without feeling looked down upon due to their financial status.

The battle of the sexes

Men and women have always shared a certain antagonism since sin entered the picture. Nowhere has this antagonism played out like in organized religion. For years, religion has treated women as if they were second-class citizens, rejecting them the right to serve in a ministerial capacity, subjecting them to church silence or a certain dress code, and denying them access to rites and ceremonies. Even though there are those who insist on continuing this battle today with all sorts of Scriptural misrepresentations and defenses, no one can debate or argue the meaning of Galatians 3:28-29: *There is neither Jew nor Greek, there is neither bond nor free, there is neither male nor female: for ye are all one in Christ Jesus. And if ye be Christ's, then are ye Abraham's seed, and heirs according to the promise.* (KJV) If we are all one in Christ Jesus and all heirs to the promise, that means male and female alike are invited to be participants in that promise. The Word does not segregate men and women to separate but equal roles or into master and servant. Those classes between men and women are the creation of men and have been rightly destroyed by Christ. Church, let's move past this pettiness and on to the glory in Christ!

"Christian racism"

Anyone who has studied the Scriptures thoroughly knows this statement is an oxymoron. There are many, however, who have made it a life's work to distort the precious Word of God and turn it into a code for racist propaganda. Through means such as television and the internet, white supremacists who claim to come in the Name of Christ spread their message of segregation and hatred to millions worldwide. Even though many brand their rhetoric as total nonsense, the natural assumption that everyone feels this way breeds a dangerous silence.

In ancient times, there was great competition between nations - not so much in a racial sense - but in the sense of which nation was more powerful. A nation able to conquer and overtake another nation was deemed more powerful, and those who lost the battle were enslaved. This ancient game of power and control caused ethnic groups to rival one another which eventually, over time, became racial stereotypes.

We are called to a far higher standard than meager power trips to assess and characterize people. In Matthew 12:48-50, Jesus breaks down a powerful racial barrier with His words: *He replied to him, 'Who is My mother, and who are My brothers?' Pointing to His disciples, He said, 'Here are My mother and My brothers. For whoever does the will of My Father in heaven is My brother and sister and mother.'* Those who are Christians (doing the will of the Father) are brothers and sisters in Christ, despite their ethnic origins. Once we are called into the one new man, we are never the same. While we may still look different on the outside, God has performed the same sanctifying work within us that has given us life and love in Him. We need to recognize this fact as an essential part of the Gospel because Jesus did not command us to just go out and preach the Gospel to our own race, but to the entire world. In and of itself, the Gospel could rightly be considered the first integration action!

The modern thing to do in church is divide into smaller classes and be known by ethnicity. Sometimes we need a reminder that we are not called to have a partitioned church: there is no white church, black church, Hispanic church, Chinese church, or other ethnic grouping of churches. Everyone who is a part of the Body of Christ is commanded to be welcoming to all who come through their doors and to work with all who set forth to live for the Kingdom and walk in the footsteps of Jesus Christ. When faced with the work of Christ, ethnicity and race do not matter to God, so they should not matter to us.

> **AUTHOR'S REFLECTIONS**
>
> Church unity isn't just a nice musing for songs or for parting words in a sermon to make people feel better about themselves or all warm and fuzzy. The principle is not something that operates as a council or a musing for a committee. Christian unity starts with genuine love for one another and a genuine desire to work with others in the advance of the Gospel. When – and only when – we reach this point will we see the unity of the church as an achievable goal.

Does the Bible support slavery?

There is a growing group of men who, claiming to be Christian, believe we need to reinstitute slavery as a necessary class in society. To such men, they feel the answer of debt and repayment is solved if we will only go back to a system that endorses slavery. Their argument? The Bible not only advocates slavery, it is a part of the Christian way!

Slavery is an intricate and dark aspect of human history. Slaves became slaves by a number of different methods: through criminal behavior, becoming prisoners of war, losing a battle, incurring debt, or being born into a family that was enslaved. Slaves also had a number of ways in which they could leave a life of slavery: by working long enough to pay off their debt, by having a relative financially cover their release, or by the kindness of their masters. More modern concepts of slavery are not quite as cut and dry. Many instances of modern slavery include kidnapping, bribery, people turning on their own, greed, and forced servanthood that was impossible to get out of.

While slavery is mentioned in the Bible (as it was a part of ancient system), there is nothing in the Scriptures which condones slavery or suggests it is the most viable answer to problems of debt or financial ruin. Even though the story of Onesimus, the runaway slave who the Apostle Paul instructs to return to his master, is long cited as a justification for slavery, the book of Philemon is not an across-the-board philosophical tome on enslavement. We do not know the situation which existed between Onesimus and his master; but we can assume from the letter and other injunctions for believers to pay their debts that Onesimus owed Philemon a debt and that had to be paid. As slavery was the method of payment, that is how Onesimus had to cover his debt. If Paul were writing to people today, the injunction would be not to run from debt, but to pay what is owed. Re-instituting slavery is not the answer to deterring debt or crime; we need to work to promote change in the hearts of men and women that will solve these problems rather than try to deter people away from them.

A classless Kingdom

The purpose of class distinctions is to make it easier to distinguish who is more desirable for socialization, social advancement, and social prestige based on criteria of financial wealth, family name, social associations, sex, and race. The Kingdom of God represents the sole society that has ever stood without class distinctions. In a world where we are told that dividing into class is not only inevitable but necessary, Christianity has the unique job of proving the world wrong. We can live without judging people by their income, race, sex, or mistakes. We need to remember that when Jesus died, He died for the sins of the whole world. He did not look upon the social classes of humanity and decided to only die for some. We, in turn, must live in a similar way. While ministry and church life may feel a lot like junior high at times, with its cliques, groups, and expectations, we aren't called to live in such immaturity as we bear the Name of Christ. And sometimes we need a bold reminder to bring us back to reality: church and ministry are not about our shoes, where we are from, how much money we have, our sex, our race, our family name, or our social connections; being a Christian is about Who we know - God the Father through our Lord and Savior Jesus Christ!

Apostle Marino preaching in Florence, South Carolina (May 2009)

10 DISCERNING WISE AND FOOLISH BEHAVIOR
(Volume 11, Number 4 – July/August 2012)

Recently the Lord began calling one of the women covered by my ministry to start hosting "Midnight Oil Prayer" periodically. When she spoke about why she was called to this, the wise and foolish virgins came up. In speaking of that, I realized that the reason why midnight prayer and the virgins were so inter-connected on that prayer call. The first reason is because these are the "last days," and that, thereby, makes it the "midnight hour." It means that the coming of Jesus is nearer than when we first believed, and near enough to which we need to take our times and our awareness of His coming seriously. The second part of that plays in with the first: if it is the midnight hour, then the wise virgins are called to be ready at any time, as the Groom will come. Yet the Word cautions us greatly against the foolish - and for good reason, as He has revealed on tonight. As I read the passage after we got off the prayer line, I realized something very key: there is only one way to be wise, but many ways to be foolish. The way we tell the difference is by discernment: discerning wise and foolish behavior.

Words on the fifty/fifty Kingdom of God

"Then the kingdom of heaven shall be likened to ten virgins who took their lamps and went to meet the bridegroom. Five of them were foolish (thoughtless, without forethought) and five were wise (sensible, intelligent, and prudent)." (Matthew 25:1-2, AMPC)

I've heard so many spins on what this passage is about, it isn't funny. The Word is clear that it is the Kingdom of God; in other words, it is about us. In the Kingdom of God, there are, therefore, both foolish people and wise people. In fact, the Word here points out that the numbers are about half and half: half of us are wise, and half of us are foolish. How many of you have heard me lament about how many people just act like idiots? Well, I'm not that far off the mark. If 50% of the church is foolish, that means the dingbat ratio is enough to make someone nuts.

This does beg the question, however: why are there foolish people in the Kingdom? If the Bible exalts wisdom, why would God tolerate foolishness? My best answer to this question is that there are three possibilities, and I'm still not sure there is not more to possibly glean from it. The first answer is to say that salvation isn't based on our personal level of wisdom. There are many, many wise people throughout history who over-relied on wisdom and became vain in that knowledge. The second reason is because we live in a foolish age, where even the church is foolish. With ministers who don't teach right and people who don't discern right, it's not a big secret that wisdom isn't a prime value in today's church. Believers think if they get a new car, God must be happy with them, failing to consider the fact that anyone can go and get a car loan and have a car. They don't know wisdom because it isn't a value; that which is wise is deemed complicated or unnecessary in favor of often what could be deemed as that which is ridiculous. It's also worth noting (as something I tapped on in a recent blog) that not everything in the Word or even in the Christian life is about salvation. One of the biggest mistakes we make in today's church is turning everything into a heaven/hell debate. The Apostle Paul points out that while all things may be permitted, not all things are beneficial. The Apostle pointed out with his very words that not everything is a salvation

> **BEHIND THE ARTICLE**
>
> My thoughts on wise and foolish behavior started out as a blog first, rather than an article followed by a blog (which is a bit unusual for me). I felt the topic was so important, however, that I made sure I took the time to do an article on it, as well. When it comes to wisdom and foolishness, I don't think we always think of it in such practical terms. This is why examination of both is so crucial according to Scripture.

issue - some things are just about the exercise of wisdom. Smoking, for example, is not a wise decision. There are numerous reasons why smoking is a bad idea for one's health. There is nothing in the Bible, however, that says smoking is a sin. Smoking a cigarette will not keep you out of heaven. I know the body is the temple of the Holy Spirit, I know we are supposed to honor the vessel, but that is what makes smoking unwise - not a sin. Gluttony, however, is mentioned as a sin because it is about more than just physical being, and that means everyone pointing fingers at smokers better start looking at the insatiable desires they have. But, I digress. Back to the topic at hand.)

There is also the possibility that those who are in the Kingdom and are simply unwise are "tares" waiting to be revealed in this midnight hour. Because that seems to be a common theme in last days teaching, I am inclined to believe this is heavily at play in this passage. Those who are foolish grow alongside those who are wise, and, for a time, look exactly the same as those who are wise. You can't tell the difference between the two on the surface. They may go to the same church, listen to the same Christian music station, even wave their praise banners at the same time. They may both use the same ministerial "title," maybe even preach. Yet the Word here goes on to tell us how we can identify the wise from the foolish, and it is very, very simple.

The importance of setting limits and boundaries

For when the foolish took their lamps, they did not take any [extra] oil with them; But the wise took flasks of oil along with them [also] with their lamps. While the bridegroom lingered and was slow in coming, they all began nodding their heads, and they fell asleep. But at midnight there was a shout, Behold, the bridegroom! Go out to meet him! Then all those virgins got up and put their own lamps in order. And the foolish said to the wise, Give us some of your oil, for our lamps are going out. But the wise replied, There will not be enough for us and for you; go instead to the dealers and buy for yourselves. (Matthew 25:3-9, AMPC)

So the foolish didn't prepare for the bridegroom's late arrival. In other words, they just relied on the fact that he would come when THEY were ready. They believed he would do what THEY expected. They had the

---

KEY VERSE: MATTHEW 25:1-2

Then the Kingdom of Heaven shall be likened to ten virgins who took their lamps to meet the bridegroom. Five of them were foolish (thoughtless, without forethought) and five were wise (sensible, intelligent, and prudent). (AMPC)

bridegroom operating like THEY thought he should, and they made no preparations to the contrary. These are the people who today believe God works like THEY think He should. They see God as a big version of themselves: they can do no wrong, they are so "anointed," they are always dealing with the devil because it can't be that God is trying to reveal something to them, and most of all...they have a modus operandi. What exactly is that "modus operandi,' you ask?

The wise come prepared because they know God's ways are not their ways. This means that, in many ways, they are off the "beaten track." That is because they are making a new track for people to follow. They go through and face warfare in their lives, but the warfare is not haphazard: it is designed to hamper the work. In an effort to keep the lamp burning, the anointing is guarded, and extra precaution is taken to ensure the light will still be burning when Jesus returns. They persist in not falling asleep, because the journey is tiring. And what do the foolish want to do? They think that because THEY came unprepared, THEY fell asleep that they now need "help" and then they get manipulative. "Well, if you were REALLY a Christian, you'd give me some of your oil!" "If you have so much extra oil, you should share it with me!" "The Word says we should love each other; you need to show me how much you love me!" "If you are my sister/brother, you will give me some of what you got!" "You should help out my ministry with what you have - it shouldn't be about the credit!" "If the Holy Spirit is calling you to my event, you should use your own resources to get here and help me with my call!"

Don't succumb to foolish manipulation

People, people, people, the foolish are manipulative - which proves that smart they may not be, but crafty, they are! The foolish have learned enough of the ways of the Kingdom to try and use the wise to develop the call they claim God gave them. They know people aren't taught properly about matters of love and helping each other, and that ministers can easily feel guilty with the right words and presentation. The Word, however, makes it very clear what marks wisdom and what marks foolishness. The wise see through this behavior. They see through manipulative conduct and call it out for what it is. They tell them right where it's at: NO. NO, I am not going to let you suck my anointing dry because you don't have anything of your own. NO, I am not going to give you my oil because there isn't enough in me for me AND for you, too. What you need to do is go get your own.

In this day and age of ministry, there will be times when we will have to guard our anointing for dear life and not be really nice with some people. These people who try to steal our anointing, our oil, need to be told off.

They need to hear the word "NO." Yes, they will turn it and make you out to be selfish. You aren't selfish. Later in Matthew 25, Jesus does an excellent job of telling us exactly who needs our help, and it is not people who make the choice to be unprepared, lazy, pampered, self-centered, or people who want to be called but aren't, so they'll just steal what God gave to someone else. They keep trying to show up for the wedding in inappropriate clothing, just because they want to come - and God doesn't stand for it! Nobody is entitled to anything they don't pursue in God. To act any other way is to act foolishly, because letting the foolish take the anointing is to squander the gift of God on your life. So, some of us need to check ourselves and stop acting foolishly. They may be coming along to you and saying everything, and you just hand them a straw to guzzle your oil down to the point where you've got nothing left - not for God, not for anybody. Handing everyone everything they ask for is not good for them because people need to learn how to be responsible on their own. Responsibility, just as we see it in the natural, is a spiritual principle: we are spiritually responsible for ourselves and that is not learnt in the Kingdom if we hand everyone everything all the time. You are foolish to let your light go out because an anointing usurper comes along, wants what you have, and you hand it over to them. TELL THEM NO, GO GET THEIR OWN. That is what's best for them AND for you. That is wise behavior and exemplifies wisdom in a way we don't often think or consider! We can prove our wisdom by our inability to be manipulated by foolish and anointing-sucking people. No matter how wise we claim to be, we prove it when we defend the anointing God has given us for our calling.

Who misses the call of the bridegroom?

But while they were going away to buy, the bridegroom came, and those who were prepared went in with him to the marriage feast; and the door was shut. Later the other virgins also came and said, Lord, Lord, open [the door] to us! But He replied, I solemnly declare to you, I do not know you [I am not acquainted with you]. Watch therefore [give strict attention and be cautious and active], for you know neither the day nor the hour when the Son of Man will come. (Matthew 25:10-13, AMPC)

What happened here is obvious: the foolish virgins had to go off and try to prepare themselves too late. Even though they knew they were invited to the wedding, they under-prepared themselves. The fruits of their self-serving purposes are evident. The bridegroom didn't work on their timetable, so they were under prepared. In an attempt to work double-time, they came up short-sighted and missed the event they were called to be part of. Blinded by self, these people forgot to be prepared so they could watch and wait!

> **AUTHOR'S REFLECTIONS**
>
> This passage of Scripture does serve to remind us about the importance of preparation and wisdom, but it also serves to me as a reminder that even though I might feel surrounded by foolishness, there are many wise people out there, as well. As believers and especially as ministers, we should take an interest in being around people who are wise and who will help us to maintain the anointing on our lives.

Those who are foolish will miss the call of the bridegroom. They will miss the very presence of Jesus, the very wedding of the Bridegroom and the Bride spoken of in Revelation, because they will have wasted too much time trying to get something for nothing. Wisdom tells us to be prepared and to guard our preparations. In ministry, our preparations are our ministry. If we are truly chosen, our actions will align with wisdom. If we have allowed too many people to take advantage of what God has placed in our lives, now is the time to close the borders and guard what God has given. If we are foolish, it's time to check the reason for that and start being responsible. Leaders, it's time to impress responsibility on others, so they will take spiritual things seriously. Verse 13 reminds us of the importance of being alert, prepared, watchful, and waiting, because we don't know when Jesus is coming back. He could arrive ten minutes after I write this, or not for another ten thousand years. The point is that it doesn't matter. When it comes to spiritual things, we need to want and seek more than just avoiding hell after we die: we need to seek wisdom that reflects the Lord's precepts within our lives. If you are, that's great. If you're not, it's time to turn that tide...because you know not at what time the Son of Man shall return.

Are you foolish...or wise?

Of the many things I see in church today that deeply disturb me, perhaps the greatest one I see is a severe over-estimation of self. People are so preoccupied with a love of themselves - whether it manifests in their concept of being called, of what they feel they are called to do or can do, or are just so into what they want - they have totally lost sight of God. In our modern church setting, we have grown critical of the non-church world to the point of judgment. This pursuit is not a genuine separation of holiness from unholiness, it is an over-estimation of the Christian individual in pursuit of pride. We, as a church; we, as ministers; we, as those called, cannot impact the world with the gifts God has given unto us if we operate foolishly. If ministry, our call, even being a Christian has become somehow all about us, we are behaving foolishly.

2 Corinthians 4:1-7 offers us powerful perspective on ministry, and whether intentionally or not, about the power of wisdom with our anointing from God, as well: *Therefore seeing we have this ministry, as we have received mercy, we faint not; But have renounced the hidden things of dishonesty, not walking in craftiness, nor handling the word of God deceitfully; but by manifestation of the truth commending ourselves to every man's conscience in the sight of God. But if our gospel be hid, it is hid to them that are lost: In whom the god of this world hath blinded the minds of them which believe not, lest the light of the glorious gospel of Christ, Who is the image of God, should shine unto them. For we preach not ourselves, but Christ Jesus the Lord; and ourselves your servants for Jesus' sake. For God, Who commanded the light to shine out of darkness, hath shined in our hearts, to give the light of the knowledge of the glory of God in the face of Jesus Christ. But we have this treasure in earthen vessels, that the excellency of the power may be of God, and not of us.* (KJV) The excellency of what we do comes from the anointing, the unction of the Holy Spirit, God in our experience, working within and through us. If we are wise, we recognize God is working within us and we give Him the glory for all He is doing. We will guard what He has given us and will diligently work in these last days as we await the return of Jesus Christ. As earthen vessels, we will allow God to mold and shape us into what He desires us to become. As we do so, we grow in a deeper sense of wisdom and protection of the anointing deposited on our lives. Until Jesus returns, there will always be foolish people, and wise people, wheat and tares. Sometimes it will seem like the tares choose the wheat, but in the end, it will be clear that the wheat is strong and healthy, purposed for its situating as it offers nourishment with the Word of Life. On the surface, I may not be able to tell whether you are foolish or wise...until you come and ask for a portion of what I must compensate for what you don't have. In that situation, I must decide what I will do, and the type of person God has for me to become. I've made my choice. What about you? Wise or foolish - in the end, the type of person you choose to be is up to you.

Apostle Marino preaching at Sanctuary Apostolic Fellowship (later to become Sanctuary International Fellowship Tabernacle – SIFT) in Raleigh, North Carolina (January 2016)

11 SEARCHING FOR THE IMMORTAL IN ALL THE MORTAL PLACES
(Volume 6, Number 1 – January 2007)

To describe me as a "disillusioned Christian" probably would have been an understatement. While I hadn't been a Christian that long, I hadn't been a total moron far longer. In my late teens and the first year and a half of my twenties, I found myself in a total dilemma as to what to believe because so many Christians represented their faith so poorly. One too many pastors told me God personally wanted me to give them my money, and one too many congregation members blindly followed these individuals who were both ill-spirited and unscripturally motivated.

In my quest to seek something out, while I didn't totally abandon Christianity, I became particularly preoccupied with Buddhism. I read Buddhist writings; I learned about Buddhist meditation and even tried a few of them. I got the idea through listening to people within the world that Buddhism was somehow a profound, enlightened religion that had something everyone else was lacking. And while I did not believe that Buddhism had all the answers, I genuinely believed that there was a profound depth to it that I couldn't find in something else.

Reality hit home when I went on an interview to a Buddhist monastery where I spent two hours with a Buddhist nun who was neither profound nor deep, but rather a clever escape artist who found a socially acceptable way to retreat from the world. The more I listened to her, the more that disillusioned feeling returned. Not only was Buddhism not profound, but its founder also left his wife and young son to go "pursue" enlightenment, and if one really reads his words, it sounds like his pursuit was a total failure.

My confirmation on the lack of profundity in the religion came a few years later after I was past my Buddhist preoccupation phase when someone tried through excessive persuasion and pressure to get me to participate in a Zen meditation workshop without giving me the option of speaking with somebody about it first. The answer was that the only way anyone would speak to me was if I did their meditation practices first.

I was searching for the immortal in every mortal place I could find, and I didn't know it. In pursuit of God, and something that seemed to be at least somewhat of a reflection of Him, I kept leading down paths that did not lead to life but led instead to instead to death.

My experience in searching for something genuine but in every wrong place conceivable isn't uncommon. Like many people, I thought that at the very least, even if I didn't come to agree with everything that a religion taught, religion of all sorts would hold some sort of profound or immortal experience. I believed in the notion as much as anybody else that religion, in and of itself, was an end, and that by investigating, practicing, or exploring that end, I would too be able to find the answers I sought about God and about what defines right faith.

Every religion in the world makes its own promises that, ironically enough, most other religions also make. Today many people have come to a point where rather than sort through religious differences, they'll just try a little bit of everything and hopefully find something that works for them, because in making all the same claims, many people believe that all religions equally lead to God. The reasoning is that, with all claiming the same thing, and it seeming like there are equal parts of good and bad in everything, religion as a whole is a generalized expression of the same thing leading to God.

> **BEHIND THE ARTICLE**
>
> *Searching For The Immortal In All The Mortal Places* was an early sermon series of mine that examined my own journey through religion and religious study from a spiritual perspective. Inspired by a passage found in the Odes of Solomon (an apocryphal book), it was also many people's first introduction to the apocryphal writings. When I studied these writings, they often inspired many sermons and writings I would go on to do. Radical as it was to include them as an inspirational point (especially so many years ago), studying the apocrypha is an important point to learn about the history of the church and Scripture.
>
> This particular article is from a point in our history where our magazine didn't have a very fancy cover, and the editions were Xeroxed off for mailing. Unfortunately, I don't have a cover of this edition to share in this book. We are including it, regardless, because this edition reflects important aspects of *Power For Today*'s history and pursuit for truth.

I think that while this attitude may be easier to swallow for the present, it becomes more difficult to digest later, particularly as one begins picking up little bits of this and that along the way. The dichotomy of trying to be a Hindu, a Buddhist, a contemplative Christian, a Sufi Muslim, a Taoist, a Native American, and an occultist all at once creates confusion both spiritually and intellectually and also makes it so that you never know where it is you stand at any given time on many issues. In the process to find immortality through religious action, in the most mortal of places, many come to a point at the end of the journey where they feel more mortal than they ever have before.

We live in a mortal world, where everything around us eventually dies or lives itself out. Religious leaders, no matter how moral, wise, or valid they may seem, are as sinful as the rest of us and come to an end of their lives, never to return again. Over time, religious practices always change, and are modified, often without conforming to the traditional beliefs of the founders. The world changes and when beliefs become stagnant, eventually they die out. Amidst all this mortality, where is our hope?

A few years ago, while studying the apocrypha I came across the Odes of Solomon 3:8-9 which give an interesting insight into the search for immortality: *Whoever joins the immortal becomes immortal. Whoever delights in the Living One is living.*[1] These powerful words answer every question to anyone searching for God and the eternal life He offers to us in everything and everything available today. Spiritually, we are always uniting ourselves to things, and ultimately, we take on the things we unite with. If you join yourself to something that is immortal, you too, will experience eternal life. But if you join yourself unto mortality, you shall find death.

A lot of Christians today talk about the transference of an anointing. While the methods by which they talk about it can sound spooky and, well, weird, there is something in the concept that is very real and very relevant. The whole notion of spirituality is a union or agreement with certain spiritual forces: either those of God or those of Satan. While other religions tend to make the matter less simple, the reality is that every day of our lives, we are choosing to either do things that lead unto life, or things that lead unto death. In speaking of spirituality, religions that do not lead us unto Christ, the Living One, Who has paved the way for us into immortality, lead not to God, or into eternity, but lead people along what is

KEY VERSE: ISAIAH 5:20-21

Woe to those who call evil good and good evil, who put darkness for light and light for darkness, who put bitter for sweet and sweet for bitter! Woe to those who are wise in their own eyes and prudent and shrewd in their own sight! (AMPC)

often a convoluted pathway through themselves and the forces of darkness unto a unifying hold that is spiritually hard to break. When in fellowship with darkness, mortality seems as immortality, and darkness seems as light; and the longer darkness is pursued, the more unobtainable truth, life, and most especially, eternal life seems to the average, genuine seeker.

Isaiah 5:20-21 gives an interesting warning to such as who lead people who seek immortality in dark places and to those who seek it as well: *Woe to those who call evil good and good evil, who put darkness for light and light for darkness, who put bitter for sweet and sweet for bitter! Woe to those who are wise in their own eyes and prudent and shrewd in their own sight!* (AMPC) Distortions of reality cloud those who seek so much after something that many come to convince themselves that what they seek after will be found in the mortal places. The only way out of such darkness is to start seeking the immortal in the truly immortal place – which can only be found in the One Who is the Way, the Truth, and the life.

Being a Christian is totally different from anything else in the spiritual and religious realms because it offers that sweet promise of eternal life. Rather than following people who made claims they could not deliver on, our Savior proved to be the resurrection and the life. Not only did He follow through on His promises, He was also the fulfillment of the Father's promises as well, which is a claim that none other can hold. In a darkened world, clouded by lies, deceit, false religion, unity with demons, and evil, Jesus is our light, lighting us unto the way of eternal life. John 1:9-13 tells us, *There it was – the true Light [was then] coming into the world [the genuine, perfect, steadfast Light] that illumines every person. He came into the world, and though the world was made through Him, the world did not recognize Him [did not know Him]. He came to that which belonged to Him [to His own – His domain, creation, things, world], and they who were His own did not receive Him and did not welcome Him. But to as many as did receive and welcome Him, He gave the authority (power, privilege, right) to become the children of God, that is, to those who believe in (adhere to, trust in, and rely on) His Name – who owe their birth neither to bloods nor to the will of man [that of a natural father], but to God. [They are born of God!]"* (AMPC) In searching for immortality, the answer to finding that which is immortal lies in the One Who is immortal, and in His Son, the Living One, Who reigns for all eternity. The light shines for us all, and each one of us has the right to take claim of the spiritual victory eternal life has to offer. All we must do is receive the Light of life, Jesus Christ.

I know that had I received better Christian instruction, and more importantly, seen a better Christian witness that I would have never thought Christianity had nothing more to offer than anything else. If you've been following my ministry for a while, you've probably heard me say that victory is salvation this side of heaven. As eternal life is, well, eternal, that

> **AUTHOR'S REFLECTIONS**
>
> The concept of looking for eternity in places where we won't find it is not uncommon, not at all. Whenever we start thinking we've got the answer in a thing – a religion, a system, a practice, or a person – we've already lost our way. If we want to make sure we keep eternity in view, we need to make sure that we keep God as our center at all times.

indicates it affects us just as much today as it will after death or after Jesus comes back. Overcoming the things of this life that relate to mortality: fear, anxiety, spiritual insecurity, financial problems, physical problems, mental problems, relationship difficulties, depression, loneliness, sinfulness, and the like show forth that Jesus is just as real, just as alive, and just as much the overcomer He has always been to non-believers and believers alike. If we never get to the point where we overcome the mortality present in our human life through everyday living and become the super-conquerors Romans speaks of us to be, nobody can experience for themselves, both personally and by witness, all the power Jesus has invested believers with as the children of God.

Christianity is different because it leads to life every day, and in every way, through Jesus Christ, the Life Himself. No matter what is going on in our lives, we know that Jesus is risen, and we too shall be one day. Rather than trying to compete with other religions that seem popular by turning the Christian faith into a marketing machine, we need to live our faith. In this age probably more than any other people are genuinely seeking answers to problems that plague humanity in a way that they never have before, all of which relate to humanity's mortality. Therefore, the Gospel is applicable, practical, and more important to this dying world than ever before; but among many circles, it is being lost amidst politics, lawmaking, needless protests, scathing judgments, and self-righteousness. As a living people, let's display the best immortality has to offer, and not waste our time on things that shall fade when the Living One returns for a glorious, eternal church, one without unity with the mortal things of this world.

---

[1] *The Odes of Solomon* as found in *The Other Bible*, edited by Willis Barnstone. San Francisco, California: Harper Collins San Francisco, 1984.

Apostle Marino ministering during children's church at Sanctuary Apostolic Fellowship (later to become Sanctuary International Fellowship Tabernacle -SIFT) (October 2015)

12 CONFIDENT OF BETTER THINGS
(Volume 10, Number 11 – November 2011)

A common denominator in many people I encounter today is denial. Both believers and non-believers' dwell in a state where they don't deal with the realities of our world. War, famine, natural disasters, sickness, heartache, pain, and worry are all very realistic aspects in the times we are living. In order to avoid what is perceived as "negative," many people simply ignore anything they do not desire to deal with. Such a denial is, to a certain extent, explainable. Many do not understand the times in which we are living and therefore see no hope or answer for the problems that exist. Rather than get lost in an unending sea of pain and sorrow, people try to create their own escapes.

While this modern denial may be explainable, that does not mean such an attitude or approach to dealing with problems is in accordance with God's plan for us. God doesn't ask us to hold on to false hopes and ignorant concepts in the vain pursuit of self-perpetuated ignorance. What God has provided to His people instead of the need for escape is a solid promise of better things.

Sometimes the people of God need a clear reminder of these better promises God has given unto us. In some Christian communities, the message given is that the better things of God are far off, distant, and something reserved for another dimension of time. Others teach that the better things of God are reserved strictly to material things. With such extremes, it is not a wonder why people are left confused about the important things of God. If we are to excel as His people in this day and age, the better things of God are most definitely classified as "important things!"

What does it mean to be "confident" of better things? What are these better things spoken of in Scripture? How do we attain them?

Leaving behind the elementary

Recent years have seen advances of amazingly immature church movements. One such movement is the "Seeker-friendly" Movement, which places heavy emphasis on creating an atmosphere inviting to those who are not Christian, but curious about Christianity. These churches go to extreme efforts to instill comfort in their churches: ministers and members dress sloppily and casually, coffee bars and T-shirts adorn church lobbies, and church music resembles a rock concert. Preaching in such churches focuses much on God's promise and on the love of God and salvation but is notably absent about other aspects of Christian doctrine. Little is ever spoken about important and essential aspects of character and doctrinal formation. What is most noted, however, about these churches is that the members of the church are never given the opportunity to tackle even the most elementary issues in the faith. Year after year, these churchgoers are misled into thinking a relationship with God is nothing more than hearing pretty music, drinking coffee, and feeling good about themselves. Such people will never experience the better things of God, let alone reach a point of confidence in them!

> **BEHIND THE ARTICLE**
>
> I wrote this article while going through a period of "deep searching" with God. I desired to see Him in a different way, and I wasn't finding what I was looking for in the churches I visited at that time. In the process, God took me to Hebrews 6 and started showing me that the only way we grow in Him is if we are willing to leave elementary things behind.

Hebrews 6:1-3 gives us a stern word about passing from elementary teachings into deeper ones: *Therefore let us leave the elementary teachings about Christ and go on to maturity, not laying again the foundation of repentance from acts that lead to death, and of faith in God, instruction about baptisms, the laying on of hands, the resurrection of the dead, and eternal judgment. And God permitting, we will do so.* This passage of Scripture clarifies that it is essential to teach elementary teachings to new believers, that they may have a right foundation for faith; but at the same time, it is essential that believers move on to deeper teachings as they grow and develop in the faith. The basics of faith are, no doubt, important to us as believers; but we are called to resolve such issues, seeing the truth of them through solid teaching, and are called to move on to more advanced teachings. If we are to ever grow into a solid confidence and knowledge of better things in Christ, we can't be incessantly reviewing the same basic material. We are called to study the basics, know them, and then move on to everything that is deeper.

Despite this Scriptural injunction to go deeper, it is not uncommon to find entire churches and denominations hung up on the basics of faith - or even the basics of the basics of faith. As faith and salvation are both developing and deeper processes as we grow in Christ, we can never forget the importance of taking steps of developing faith into deeper spiritual matters. It is truly in the deeper areas of faith that we learn the truth of God's better promises and how to maintain our confidence in Him and all He promises to us.

Divine enlightenment

Continuing in Hebrews 6:4-8, we learn more about the process of confidence in better things: *It is impossible for those who have once been enlightened, who have tasted the heavenly gift, who have shared in the Holy Spirit, who have tasted the goodness of the word of God and the powers of the coming age, if they fall away, to be brought back to repentance, because to their loss they are crucifying the Son of God all over again and subjecting Him to public disgrace. Land that drinks in the rain often falling on it and that produces a crop useful to those for whom it is farmed receives the blessing of God. But land that produces thorns and thistles is worthless and is in danger of being cursed. In the end it will be burned.* Here we learn the precept of divine enlightenment. Divine enlightenment means we are illuminated in our minds by God's Word and His promises to us and are able to experience His revelation in our lives. Such revelation brings about practical depth to our walk: it enables the work of God to apply to us, through us, and in us as we go along. We aren't fighting God's precepts but allowing the precepts of God to speak to us.

One thing we see here that is very alerting is that those who fall away having received this divine illumination are unable to return to repentance.

KEY VERSE: HEBREWS 6:9

Even though we speak like this, dear friends, we are confident of better things in your case – things that accompany salvation.

Why would this clause stand here as we are discussing better promises? Rejecting the enlightenment of God comes with consequences. We can't shirk off what God has revealed to us in disobedience and hope to receive the same benefits as those who receive. If rejection of divine revelation was an acceptable course, it would require Jesus' sacrifice be continually remade to compensate for wrongdoing. All throughout the Scriptures we see clear evidence that God does not force us to follow His ways - and growing deeper in Him is no exception. The enlightenment of God prompts us to greater obedience, not a rejection of His ways and precepts.

In this vain, Hebrews 6 reiterates the importance of being a metaphorical "fertile ground." We are to act upon the divine revelation we receive from Him as such revelation is a part of God's revealed better things. As we pray and seek God, it is unrealistic to think we can just waste what He gives us. Those who reject this revelation and fail to come to bear fruit will reap their own harvest and not live in the blessings of the Kingdom. But for those of us who receive God's revelation, we will continue to trust for better things!

Avoiding laziness in pursuit of better things

There are many things God's Word advises us to avoid as we follow the Christian life. Hebrews 6:9-12 advises us: *Even though we speak like this, dear friends, we are confident of better things in your case—things that accompany salvation. God is not unjust; He will not forget your work and the love you have shown Him as you have helped His people and continue to help them. We want each of you to show this same diligence to the very end, in order to make your hope sure. We do not want you to become lazy, but to imitate those who through faith and patience inherit what has been promised.* It's obvious God desires us to pursue the things which accompany salvation - everything in His Word that pertains to the abundant life. However, we must recognize the call to pursue those good things. God's ways do not just fall into our lap but pertain to our pursuit of His ways and our obedience to Him. It is plain to see as we do good, God is aware of all we do in His Name with a productive and useful end. The people of God are to avoid laziness and seek that which is right, noble, and true in their work.

Why is there a specific injunction to avoid laziness? Clearly any doctrine can be perverted to take personal responsibility and works out of it. Numerous doctrines remove personal responsibility in an effort to find a balance between faith and works. While the system of working for one's salvation is incompatible with the saving grace of Christ on the cross, living our faith in such a way that our faith in Christ shows is not incompatible! All throughout salvation history we see examples of people who displayed their faith through obedience and action. Imitating such faith does not mean we simply hope for better things but display our hope through active confidence. Proverbs 6:6-8 gives confirming words on diligence, as is found in one of God's smallest creatures: *Go to the ant, you sluggard; consider its ways and be wise! It has no commander, no overseer or ruler, yet it stores its provisions in summer and gathers its food at harvest."* Our model for diligence comes from the ant, which labors and works tirelessly, both for the good of the colony and for itself as an individual. It doesn't need to be reminded of what needs to be done, but it simply addresses it and does it. In turn, we are to be like an ant: we are to be diligent in doing good, helping others and working together for the good of the Kingdom community, and continuing in productive provision. Faith breeds diligence, not laziness! True believers will not be content with a lazy life but will be confident that all God has promised will come to pass as they wait with diligent hope and action.

Patience as we wait on promises

The majority of people in this world have a difficult time with patience. We want what we want when we want it, if not sooner. There are even those who forego receiving from God in favor of receiving something immediate which is not part of the promise. This disturbing trend is due to impatience. I think we often fail to recognize that people of faith, despite whatever age they might have lived throughout salvation history, all had one thing in common: they all spent a lot of time waiting on God. Hebrews 6:13-15 affirms the process of waiting involved in faith: *When God made His promise to Abraham, since there was no one greater for Him to swear by, He swore by Himself, saying, "I will surely bless you and give you many descendants." And so after waiting patiently, Abraham received what was promised."* Just as God promised to Abraham, so He promises to us as well; and just like Abraham, we have to wait for the manifestation. Sometimes it pays for us to examine the length of time people had to wait for their promises to manifest. Abraham, for example, had to wait ten years for Isaac, the child of promise, to manifest. Moses was over eighty years of age when he was called to stand before Pharaoh. When we are in times of waiting for the promises of God to manifest, we can remember that even great heroes of faith had to wait as well. It is most important, regardless of how long we must wait, that we remember God is faithful to all He has said and will be faithful to fulfill His promises in our situations as well.

In the meantime, we are called to wait with patience on the promises of God. Patience doesn't mean doing nothing but wait, but commands we continue in the things of God with all diligence and seek God even greater as we trust in Him. For ten years Abraham developed his faith and prepared to receive that promise, just as we are all called to do.

Kingdom living is deeper than the surface

> **AUTHOR'S REFLECTIONS**
>
> The temptation to go over the elementary things of faith repeatedly exists because those early assurances make us feel good and reassured in the faith. When it comes to going deeper in God, the process doesn't always feel good. We deal with rejection, trials, challenges, and changes that we don't always expect. That's why it is important to hold on to the elementary assurances we find in our faith: they carry us foundationally throughout our spiritual growth and development process.

The promise of better things made in the Scriptures is much deeper than just trusting God for material things. Even though much of church talk centers around how to get things or get what one wants from God, living confident for all that God has for us encompasses a much deeper way than seeking things which bring surface happiness. Luke 17:20-21 reiterates: *And when He was demanded of the Pharisees, when the kingdom of God should come, He answered them and said, The Kingdom of God cometh not with observation: Neither shall they say, Lo here! or, lo there! for, behold, the Kingdom of God is within you.* (KJV) The promise of the Kingdom of God within us causes a powerful realization: this life is more than about us and what we can get from it. As believers, we have the sacred deposit of the Kingdom living within, among, and around us wherever we go. While God does promise to provide for us in the material, we can never forget that some of what God promises to us are all things we cannot see as long as we walk in this world. Though we can see the manifestations of the Spirit, we can't see the Holy Spirit in and of Himself in this life although He has been promised to be with us and intercede for us. We are promised heaven, but heaven is a realm beyond what we can see in this world. We can't see Jesus living right now as He is in heaven, but that doesn't mean we are any less confidence in His saving power, alive and with us just as much as it has ever been. If we can't trust God to meet every promise, we CAN eventually see this side of heaven, how can we say we trust God for the promises we won't be able to see in the natural?

Why trust in the promises of God?

As we covered in the beginning of this article, the world does not make nor keep its promises well. When believers are faced with the realities of this life, the bleakness of human existence without God, and the meaninglessness of life without direction, it makes us realize the promises of God have been given to us as a grace to hold on as we go through our lives. We need to focus more deeply on that which is truly important instead of getting caught up in the complexities of life which lead to nothing but despair and disappointment. 2 Corinthians 1:18-22 affirms the fact that God's promises are sure and secure: *But as surely as God is faithful, our message to you is not 'Yes' and 'No.' For the Son of God, Jesus Christ, Who was preached among you by me and Silas and Timothy, was not 'Yes' and 'No,' but in Him it has always been "Yes.' For no matter how many promises God has made, they are 'Yes' in Christ. And so through Him the 'Amen' is spoken by us to the glory of God. Now it is God who makes both us and you stand firm in Christ. He anointed us, set His seal of ownership on us, and put His Spirit in our hearts as a deposit, guaranteeing what is to come.* We can take confidence that every promise of God is secure as He has sealed us, anointed us, and placed His Spirit within us to affirm our confidence in Him. In God through Christ, we never have to worry that He will change His mind, steer us in the wrong direction, or have bad intentions at heart. All we have to do is trust and remain confident that God will be faithful to all He has promised as we are faithful to Him and stay the course to inherit every promise throughout our days with Him.

Where are you with the promises of God? Are you confident of better things, or are you still struggling to gain insight past the basics? Wherever you are, recognize that what God has to come is so much better than right now, and make that effort to gain confidence as God reveals His true plan of better promises ahead for you!

Apostle Marino ministering during children's church a minister's ordination in Tucson, Arizona (October 2013)

13 REPRESENTING CHRIST
(Volume 12, Number 4 – May/June 2013)

Differing religious denominations and traditions have different doctrines and precepts about what can "represent" the divine in their understanding.

To some, they embrace the concept of becoming enlightened through years of meditation and good practices. If they do this enough, they can become a good representation of the highest good available to mankind and, hopefully, achieve a spiritual understanding otherwise unobtainable.

Others believe it's important to work out past negative actions and beliefs by being very good at what one does, right now. They believe they are forever being punished for what they once did and hope to obtain an understanding of the divine that will lead them to a better life, either in the immediate future or sometimes in other lifetimes from now.

Traditional Jewish belief teaches that one manifests divine representation through obedience to the law. We can see from Bible history that this attempt toward divine manifestation did not work successfully and met with many hardened hearts and disobedient factions. Nonetheless, there are many Jews today who have abandoned such traditional notions of obedience and now accept all sorts of beliefs, characters, and philosophies as evidence of divine manifestation in one's life.

Muslims across the board agree they can best represent their concept of divinity by obedience to the Koran and their prophet, Mohammed. Beyond this commonality, Muslims disagree about how this can be best achieved. Due to disagreements of Koranic interpretation, Muslim groups often fight with each other about what is the best way to manifest the Islamic life.

The list of ways different groups believe the divine is represented in their belief system is literally endless. Each group and nuance of differential belief within each sector brings out a new light to how the divine of their doctrine can manifest. In viewing this list, traditional religious viewpoints of Christianity aren't much better in their unity about how we manifest the true Divinity found in the Word made flesh than other religions are in trying to explain their own experience with their beliefs about the divine. With different groups believing different things, the concept of how to represent Christ (God the Father's ultimate divine reaching out to mankind) becomes muddled and even confusing. What does it mean to "represent" Christ? Is that the job of all Christians, or only a few? Better yet, how do we represent Christ in a world hostile to Him? In true Christian teaching, how does the Word reveal that we represent Christ to the world?

> **BEHIND THE ARTICLE**
>
> When it came time to write an article for this edition, I wanted to write something about the nature of Christ without being real theological or preachy. The result was an examination in our call to represent – or re-present – Christ to the world.

Let us put on Christ

Romans 6:1-10 provides deep insight into the power of our baptism: *What shall we say, then? Shall we go on sinning so that grace may increase? By no means! We died to sin; how can we live in it any longer? Or don't you know that all of us who were baptized into Christ Jesus were baptized into his death? We were therefore buried with Him through baptism into death in order that, just as Christ was raised from the dead through the glory of the Father, we too may live a new life. If we have been united with Him like this in His death, we will certainly also be united with Him in his resurrection. For we know that our old self was crucified with Him so that the body of sin might be done away with, that we should no longer be slaves to sin— because anyone who has died has been freed from sin. Now if we died with Christ, we believe that we will also live with Him. For we know that since Christ was raised from the dead, He cannot die again; death no longer has mastery over Him. The death He died, He died to sin once for all; but the life He lives, He lives to God.* Clearly the Word teaches us that as we are united to Christ in baptism, so truly do we signify the death we have to the flesh and sin and the rising to new life in Him. Our purpose in becoming a Christian is to die to ourselves and put on the life of Christ, that He may live in us.

If we are putting on the nature of Christ, that makes us the representatives of Christ this side of heaven. When we go out, people should see His glorious nature at work in and through us rather than seeing the tirades of the flesh at every turn. It also means that Christian representation of the divine is different than it is in other religions. Rather than attempting to become something, we unite ourselves to Christ and die to the sinful nature. While religious systems try to bring about holiness and godliness through rules, we acknowledge that the nature comes from Christ Himself as we conform ourselves into the likeness of His death and resurrection. Since we have put on Christ, we must conform to the will of God in a deeper way than the mere legalism of following rules.

Re-presenting Christ, part 1

The word "represent" literally divides into a main word and a prefix: "re" and "present." This gives two interpretations for what the word "represent" means. The first interpretation is to make now present something from before or someone who cannot be present now. In this understanding, representing Christ means that we literally stand to make His presence real, living, and known today. As Jesus is not currently with us in bodily form on earth, we become the representatives of Christ through our lives and witness while we are here.

In Acts 1:8, Jesus issues the following decree: *But you will receive power when the Holy Spirit comes on you; and you will be My witnesses in Jerusalem, and in all Judea and Samaria, and to the ends of the earth.* The reality of this world is that many people are unwilling to take the time to sit and listen to the Gospel message from start to finish. Most people are unwilling to devote hours of study to truly learn about the Word if they have little to no knowledge of it prior. This means that the people who claim to know God, the power of Christ's resurrection, and the Word of God become highly relevant in the non-Christian's perception of Who Christ is. We are endowed with power to represent Christ and point the way to God

---

KEY VERSE: ACTS 1:8

But you will receive power when the Holy Spirit comes on you; and you will be My witnesses in Jerusalem, and in all Judea and Samaria, and to the ends of the earth.

in a positive and life-affirming manner. This is our spiritual deposit given through the unction of the Holy Ghost. We do not receive the Holy Ghost to feel good or puff ourselves up, but to proclaim the Gospel to the world through both our actions and whatever calling we have as we live the Christian life.

Many people believe Jesus is distant or far-off because they cannot reach out and touch Him. They argue incessantly that Christians would live and act differently if Jesus were among them physically, and that this therefore makes Christianity dishonest. There is only one answer to this solution: to re-present Christ, representing Him with the Holy Ghost living inside of us. Matthew 5:14-16 reaffirms this call: *You are the light of the world. A city on a hill cannot be hidden. Neither do people light a lamp and put it under a bowl. Instead they put it on its stand, and it gives light to everyone in the house. In the same way, let your light shine before men, that they may see your good deeds and praise your Father in heaven.* Jesus is here among us in Spirit and in the lives, testaments, and character of His faithful. We are not here for nothing!

Re-presenting Christ, part 2

The second part of "re-presenting" Christ involves making Christ present again. This means that Christ was present in someone's life at another time and is not now. It also refers to re-presenting Christ to those who have received a false doctrine or impression of Who He is. Just because someone claims to be a believer in Jesus Christ does not mean that they are indeed believing in Jesus correctly or that they have received the truth about relationship with Him. Millions of people attend services in dead churches which provide stories about Jesus, making Him no more than a leading character in events playing out thousands of years ago. It's no wonder that many start rolling their eyes when it comes to talk of Jesus and the Father! Religion has deluded people into believing they truly know Christ when all they know is something they might have once heard about Him.

It is often difficult to present Christ to people who already think they know everything they need to know about Him. Ecumenical and interfaith movements have made it even harder to talk to people who need to know Jesus personally but don't because doctrinal differences have been watered down to the point of not mattering anymore. What was supposed to bring people together has in actuality caused more indignation and indifference - and more people needing God without even knowing it. Mark 7:6-8 warns us against teaching religious ideas as those of God: *These people honor Me with their lips, but their hearts are far from Me. They worship Me in vain; their teachings are but rules taught by men. You have let go of the commands of God and are holding on to the traditions of men.* People who hold on to false concepts of Christ need to have Him re-presented to them in true believers who by the Spirit tear down religious strongholds and mindsets.

As was mentioned earlier, re-presenting Christ also means bringing Him to people who had Christ present with them once, but who have now pushed that presence away. Some call these people "backsliders:" people who were once active in faith, but "slid back" into sin. The reasons why people depart from the presence of Christ in their lives are many and varied, and often many complain of the negative representation of others in their decision to depart from faith. It makes it all the more relevant for us to stand as representatives of Christ, truly showing His heart to the world. Let us not forget Isaiah 43:10: *"You are my witnesses," declares the LORD, "and My Servant Whom I have chosen, so that you may know and believe Me and understand that I am He. Before Me no god was formed, nor will there be one after Me."* This is the essence of "re-presenting" Christ!

A divine responsibility

The church today likes to talk a lot about the benefits of believing and professing Christian faith. What we never hear about is that with benefits first comes great responsibility. If we want to receive the benefits, we must first apply the precepts to execute our responsibilities.

One would think, from the emphasis on benefits, that being a Christian and therefore a representative of Christ are easy precepts. The truth is that being a Christian is not as easy as sitting back and receiving endless amounts of material things from God. What is involved in Christian responsibility? There are five major areas that every Christian needs to attend to as solid representatives of Christ:

- **Obedience to God** - *Hear now, O Israel, the decrees and laws I am about to teach you. Follow them so that you may live and may go in and take possession of the land that the LORD, the God of your fathers, is giving you.* (Deuteronomy 4:1) Ever since the beginning, obedience to God has been a prime cornerstone of belief and integrity when following God. No one can call themselves a follower of Christ or a "little Christ," as the word "Christian" literally means, and live in disobedience to God. Christ's representation of the Father demonstrated the ultimate obedience and emptying of personal will for the sake of the Father's will. Representing Christ means we do the same: we empty ourselves in obedience to Christ and the Father. Do you want to be a good representative of Christ? Then you must come to know God's will and obey God.

> **AUTHOR'S REFLECTIONS**
>
> I once heard someone say that you might be the only Bible that some people ever read. It can be challenging, if impossible, to get some people to give Jesus a chance because of how they feel other people have represented Him. Making sure that you do not discredit the faith and the work of Christ should be of prime thought in the life of every believer.

- **Integrity** - It has been said that "Integrity means doing the right thing when no one is looking." While many people believe that following God is about how things appear on the outside, any true representative of Christ recognizes that what we do when no one sees us is just as important as what we do in the presence of many. Psalm 25:21 reminds us of the importance of walking in integrity: *May integrity and uprightness protect me, because my hope is in You.* Integrity is a protection for us! It keeps us from wild rumors and nonsense spreading which can ruin our reputations and tarnish the image people have of us as we represent Christ. The Christian life would be much simpler to follow if people would live by integrity and stop having to cover up tracks for misdeeds or inappropriate behavior. Do we want to represent Christ? We have to make sure our behavior is consistent across the board, to everyone we encounter.

- **Spiritual power** - We don't hear much about spiritual power today because many denominations have limited the Holy Spirit's activity in this modern age. The result of such a limitation changes our perception of what the Spirit can do in our lives to an inactive state. The Word of God does not call for such inactivity, but states to us: *Behold, I have given you authority and power...* (Luke 10:19, AMPC) God has not sent us to this world and then left us ill-equipped for our call to divine representation. We must draw on the spiritual power we have to walk as representatives of Christ in this lost world.

- **Prayer/devotion** - It's amazing how shallow or nonexistent the prayer lives of many are today. If people aren't praying for things, they aren't praying at all. If we do not understand prayer as our communication with God, we will abandon prayer and turning it instead into a grocery list of needs and wants we believe God should answer. Ephesians 6:18 gives us a key for strong prayer in the representing life: *And pray in the Spirit on all occasions with all kinds of prayers and requests. With this in mind, be alert and always keep on praying for all the saints.* Prayer is not just about voicing needs but about praying in the Spirit on a level of communication beyond what may rest or lie in the natural. It is a source of sharing, where we release what is spiritual within and receive what is spiritual from above. The world is not going to be impressed by prayers from a book, but it will be impressed by the transformation within you of true prayer and devotion in your life.

- **A strong relationship with Christ** - We can't represent Christ if we do not know Him. Just as our human relationships with one another must be nurtured and cultivated, so too must our relationship with Christ. While many erroneously believe that establishing a relationship with Christ is the high point of a believer's life, it is truly the development of that relationship which grows and strengthens over time that displays great fruit. We cannot claim to be strong in faith and great representatives of Christ if we do not know Him for ourselves personally, experiencing the power of loving and knowing Him in our everyday lives. 1 Corinthians 2:16 reminds us: *...but we have the mind of Christ.* We can only claim such as we walk with Him and know Him.

Changing minds

The call to evangelize any generation is not an easy one. The difficulties and rejections from the world can create obstacles everywhere we turn. The world is simply waiting for the church to screw up so it can point and say, "SEE - IT IS WRONG!" With so many odds, it is not just a good idea, but a very imperative necessity for us to stand as good representatives of Christ. We need to re-present Him as living and active and represent Him correctly according to Who He has revealed Himself to be in the Word. It is only when those who call themselves Christians get their act together that things will begin to change in the realm of changing the minds of non-believers. John 1:14 comes alive again: *The Word became flesh and made His dwelling among us. We have seen His glory, the glory of the One and Only, Who came from the Father, full of grace and truth.* We are given the awesome responsibility and blessing to point to the One Who is the Way, the Truth, and the Life to the Father. Then and only then, as we stand as His witnesses, re-presenting Christ, will we see others begin to receive of the grace and truth of our Lord Jesus Christ.

Apostle Marino posing for a picture after recording a video blog at Sanctuary International Fellowship Tabernacle -SIFT in Raleigh, North Carolina (May 2016)

14 MOVING UP HIGHER!
(Volume 8, Number 10 – October 2009)

For years and years I waited for God to bring things to pass in my life. I would sit and pray and exhort and beg God for whatever it was that I thought I wanted. I would spend nights crying and telling God this was just all too hard and that I would just up and die if He didn't do something for me. Then when God didn't bend to my will at that moment, I would pout and get mad at God and ignore Him for a few days, telling Him to go and find someone else to ignore. After about a week of this, I would apologize to God and feel all bad only until something else didn't go my way, which would often be an issue within a few days. I lived in a circle, going around and around the mountain another time, acting childish and pouting for years at a time. In between the pouting, I would wait for God to make His move and wave His magical wand to get me out of the wilderness and into the Promised Land. I guess my logic was that I would just wake up one morning after going to bed in reality and arise in the land where the elves and the faeries take care of people, with no problems, no people to get on my nerves, no stress factors, no financial woes, no lack of support, and no past to haunt me or have to overcome any longer. I literally thought "moving up higher" meant that God would take me to a new level, truly out of this world. Little did I know, God wanted to take me to a new level that was far above where I was. He wanted to reveal to me His wisdom, His insights, and the depths of His spirituality. What I also failed to realize is that God could not elevate me to where He wanted me to be until I was ready to be lifted to that level.

Wilderness realizations

Apparently, my feeling that God owed me a promotion wasn't a new problem. I remember reading the story of the Hebrews while they were in the wilderness one day a few years ago and realizing just how they must have sounded. Scripture indicates an awful lot of complaining went on out there in the wilderness. What must they have sounded like? "I am soooo tired of this manna! All we ever get to eat is manna, manna, MANNA!" "I do not like this water from this rock; I am sick of water pouring forth from this rock! I want water from a faucet in a glass!" "I am sick of water, where is my beer?!" "What is with this quail, I wanted chicken!" "What did God mean, sending us out here in the wilderness? We were better off in slavery, where we used to be!" "Man, I miss Egypt - at least we had more choice in what we could eat!" They sounded like such ingrates!

They sounded like me. Like any one of us when we get it in our minds that God owes us something new, different, or more profound in our lives than what we have now. Sometimes I think we get this notion that God is our butler and every time we make a request of Him, He should answer us with, "You rang?" and then get right on our requests in the manner we deem most efficient, right, and best. We don't like to wait, and society is constantly creating more and more ways, so we don't have to wait for anything. We have drive-through pharmacies, restaurants, the ability to send letters and messages via the click of a computer mouse, and as the world continues to speed up, we expect even more drive-through service from God. We think we are ready for our promotion when we want it, we want it then and there, and better yet, obtaining it should be easy. And in this quest to find the easy way to promotion and the easy way to growth and elevation, we fail to realize one key thing: we are often the only thing standing in the way of our

> **BEHIND THE ARTICLE**
>
> *Moving Up Higher!* Was the first article that ever appeared in *Power For Today* Magazine that expounded upon my own personal walk with God. Prior to this article, which appeared numerous times over an eight-year span, I spoke from a strict doctrinal perspective rather than a personal one. This unique article gave our readers insight not just into spiritual realities, but of some of the personal struggles we have as we grow into our callings as ministers of the Gospel. For many of our readers, it was the first time they ever had a minister admit they had issues within their relationship with God.

progress. No doubt, God plays a part in our promotion, in getting us out of the wilderness and into our Promised Land. We too, however, play a role in our own promotion. We can't move up higher until we are fully ready for all that promotion will bring to our lives. God lifts us up, but He always asks us to reach up to meet Him as we do our part.

Is it taking you forty years to make an eleven-day trip?

Many people are unaware that the journey through the wilderness, spoken of in Deuteronomy 1:2, should have taken eleven days. It wasn't meant to be a forty-year trip, which is how long the Hebrews wandered around out there, going around and around and around the same mountain over and over and over again. Why did they keep wandering around out there? No, the reason is not because they didn't want to ask for directions or forgot to bring the map from Egypt! I believe the Hebrews expected a free ride and their own stubbornness, unwillingness to learn and mature, and their unwillingness to go in and take the Promised Land (it wasn't just going to be handed over to them) shows us that they just hadn't moved up to a level where they were ready to do all that. Deuteronomy 1:6-8 recounts God's command to the Hebrews to take the Promised Land and note the wording: God gave them the land, but they had to go in and take it for themselves: *The Lord our God said to us in Horeb, You have dwelt long enough on this mountain. Turn and take up your journey and go to the hill country of the Amorites, and to all their neighbors in the Arabah, in the hill country, in the lowland, in the south (the Negeb), and on the coast, the land of the Canaanites, and Lebanon, as far as the great river, the river Euphrates. Behold, I have set the land before you; go in and take possession of the land which the Lord swore to your fathers, to Abraham, to Isaac, and to Jacob, to give to them and to their descendants after them.* (AMPC) In other words, the Hebrews had to reach out and claim what God gave them; it was not a simple matter of God paratrooping them into the Promised Land. Just as God had to keep His promise and reach out to the Hebrews with their inheritance, so too the Hebrews had to keep their promise to reach out to God. Their promotion into the Promised Land was literally just that - a promotion. They had to earn it. The same is true with our promotions in the Lord today; we have to reach out to God and obey Him in order to experience promotion. The Hebrews were supposed to learn

---

KEY VERSE: DEUTERONOMY 1:6

The Lord our God said to us in Horeb, You have dwelt long enough on this mountain.
(AMPC)

enough, receive enough, and grow enough in the wilderness to be prepared to take the Promised Land. We must realize our wilderness experiences are not just time passed complaining, whining, and waiting for something better, but like all things with God, our time in the wilderness has a deeper purpose.

Cleaning up our wilderness act

Our examination of the "wilderness" experience of different individuals in Scripture shows us how we can help ourselves to move up higher rather than walk around that mountain yet another time. It also shows us how we can hinder ourselves if we choose the spin around the mountain rather than moving toward the Promised Land. There are a few key factors we need to watch for while waiting for promotion, and we shall look at some of them here.

Commitment to God

This is probably one of the biggest blocks for individuals who desire to move up higher, but don't seem to be getting anywhere. Whenever things become difficult in their lives, and sometimes even when things are easy, the temptation to fall away from God always exists. The entire Old Testament proves to us that when the old covenant people went through either trying times or abundant times, they were always tempted to move away from God. More often than not, they fell into the temptation, only to create more problems for themselves. Often people who fall away from God find their commitment to God in regulations and rules, thinking that devotion to God lies in observing rules and regulation rather than in loving God and obeying Him out of that loving relationship. It's a fact: if we don't worship God while in the valley, we won't worship God on the mountain. Our wilderness experiences are designed to make it so we realize how much we need God in our lives and how much He loves us and genuinely wants to give us. The opposite experience was true of Job who, despite forty years of turmoil, hardship, and loss, turned more to God than away from Him. After Job's wilderness experience, he received his Promised Land, seven times more abundant than what he started with! It's so important that during our wilderness years we seek God with the same intensity that we think we would have if God promoted us to where we desire to be then and there. That means we pray, seek God's will for ourselves, spend time with God in worship and praise, read and study the Scriptures to hear what God is saying to us and about us, and live in obedience to Him every step of the way. Don't think that because you haven't been promoted you are somehow exempt from living in obedience to God and from following in His precepts for life!

Attitude

I don't think it needs to be said, but I am going to say it anyway - the Hebrews had a really bad attitude while out there in the wilderness. All they did was complain about one thing or another, to the point where it irritated Moses, who in turn went and irritated God. They whined and complained to the point of obnoxious ingratitude, considering all God had done. Before becoming a Christian, the Apostle Paul had a real attitude on him, enough to make you want to reach out and smack him. Although I am not one inclined to speak of positive thinking or visualization (which is not what I am speaking of here anyway), we need to shape up and have a right attitude when dealing with God, and that means not complaining endlessly about how slow He is, or whining to Him about what is not going on in our lives. It means that we do what God instructs us to do, when He instructs us to do it, and we do so without problem or complaints. A good attitude is the difference between an individual willing to be taught and learn from God and one who stays where they are because they refuse to learn what they need to learn in order to be promoted. Even in the job realm, whiners and complainers are never promoted - and we need to see this parallel in the Kingdom as well. God is not going to promote someone always complaining about His system or ways of handling situations. We need to show ourselves capable and competent in our attitude when expecting promotion from God.

Maturity

I think many mistake maturity for legalism, which it isn't. Maturity is, in fact, the opposite of legalism. The Hebrews were excessively legalistic, but they were never mature, and this can be seen that at every turn when they thought the "supervisor" turned his or her back, they went off and carried their way into sin. If we get caught up in following many rules, we will trick ourselves into thinking we are ready for something when we won't be. Often the wilderness experience is far easier than making that move higher to promotion because as we learn and mature, more is required of us. Out there in the wilderness, God provides for us in a way that He doesn't when He knows we can provide certain things for ourselves. Deuteronomy 8:2 and 4 remind us all, *Remember how the LORD your God led you all the way in the desert these forty years, to humble you and to test you in order to know what was in your heart, whether or not you would keep His commands...Your clothes did not wear out and your feet did not swell*

> **AUTHOR'S REFLECTIONS**
>
> Sometimes I think we stay in the wilderness because we recognize that it will be harder for us to walk in the promise. Therefore, in a weird way, we avoid walking into what God has for us because we're afraid that God will expect more of us. We can't have it both ways. If we want promotion, we must expect we will be more responsible.

during these forty years. Out in the wilderness, the Hebrews enjoyed the close, connected care of God where He provided for them in a unique way. Once they entered the Promised Land, God never cared for them in this same way again. While God did continue to care for the Hebrews, it wasn't in the same exact sense extended out in the wilderness. They were to be mature enough and disciplined enough to reach out to their promotion and handle certain matters for themselves. We too will find this true in our own promotional experiences. Rule-following doesn't make us mature; living in God and placing ourselves in the center of His will makes us more mature than rules ever could.

Learning how to wait well

Much of waiting is not how long we wait, but how we wait. I acknowledge that waiting is never easy because we dwell in so much anticipation for whatever we are waiting for that we often overlook and forget the "now" quotient of the equation. Wilderness years are difficult in-between times in all of our lives as we may have moved away from some of our old bondages, but yet we aren't quite ready for all that lies ahead of us. We see the promise and the promotion, but we aren't quite able to obtain it just yet. In these times, as trite as it may sound, God does know the end from the beginning, and He does know what is best for us long-term as well as the whole picture. Whether we like to admit it or not, we will spend most of our lives with God waiting on Him to either do something, bring something to pass, bring something about in our lives, or waiting for a promotion. That means that with much of our time spent waiting, we need to pay close attention to our conduct and behavior while we wait. God isn't going to promote us before we are ready to handle all that will come to pass with our promotion - and therefore it is so important we wait with patience, hopeful expectation, and a continually right attitude throughout a wilderness experience. Romans 8:25 gives a powerful word about waiting in a wilderness season: *But if we hope for what we do not see, we wait for it with patience.* (ESV) When we live in the hope of all that God has for us that is to come, we are told that the way we are to wait is with patience rather than impatience. Impatience breeds frustration and anger; patience breeds peace.

The promise of promotion in due time

Jude 1:20-21 tells us: *But you, beloved, build yourselves up [founded] on your most holy faith [make progress, rise like an edifice higher and higher], praying in the Holy Spirit; Guard and keep yourselves in the love of God; expect and patiently wait for the mercy of our Lord Jesus Christ (the Messiah)--[which will bring you] unto life eternal.* (AMPC) These powerful words remind us that as we remain in God, we will come up in due time. We must remain in all things sensitive to the timing of God, patient in our hope and love, and encouraged in knowing God is with us and has us kept in His perfect timing. Moving up higher is a process, not the simple push of an elevator button. The sooner we come to this revelation, the easier our wait will be as we handle all things with patience.

In hindsight, I am so glad that God did not promote me to the level I thought I should be at in earlier years because I never could have handled it. No matter what I might have perceived within myself as I wandered around the mountain for yet another spin, I was not ready for promotion, and God knew that. The same is applicable for many of us who live in hopeful expectation, waiting for the promotion of God. While we may think we are ready now, if we aren't promoted now, it is because we aren't ready. There is good news, however: God does promote us when we are ready and then no force on earth can stop us from moving up higher, and then nobody can take our promotion away from us once we get there. When God moves, He moves so powerfully that it can never be undone. It's never too early or too late to start preparing to move to the next level with God. He may never be early, but God is certainly never late, either! When in doubt about receiving your promotion, remember the three young men cast in the fire because of their faith in the book of Daniel. Then remember this verse which followed: *Then the king promoted Shadrach, Meshach, and Abednego in the province of Babylon.* (Daniel 3:30). Even though they walked through the fire, they came out unharmed and were more than ready for their promotion. In due time, no matter how hard things may seem, how long they take, or what circumstances you may face, God will promote you, too!

Apostle Marino ministering in Caguas, Puerto Rico (September 2009)

15 ENJOYING YOUR SPOUSE
(Volume 12, Number 4 – July/August 2013)

The day to get married in the year 2007 was July 7. Believing in numerological superstitions, 7-7-07 was the day millions of couples all over the world rushed to the altar, hoping that being married on a date consisting of three sevens (the representation of perfection in numerology), they would have a marriage extra blessed by God. To many who are disillusioned by marriage as it exists today - almost doomed from the start in more than half of marriages - being married on what was perceived to be a perfect day seemed to equate to a perfect marriage.

The host of 7-7-07 weddings were the affairs of the year. Wedding preparations were made months in advance. The cakes were large and ornate, the bride's dress expensive and fancy, the bridesmaids all lined up and in order, and the groom and groomsmen ready in their black-tie garb. People flew into the weddings from all over the world, guests were shipped in, and wedding consultants experienced a major boom in business.

On 7-8-07, the weddings were all over. Events which took months to prepare were over after a few hours, at most. The focus for months and months was on the wedding, rather than the marriage. The centerpieces were taken home, the dress went back to the closet, the guests all returned home, and eventually each couple married on July 7, 2007 was faced with the prospect of real life. Whether or not these couples are happy, I don't know. Whether or not these couples will stay together, I don't know. But what I do know is that for any marriage to last, it must pass from being about the wedding fantasies to the actual relationship a couple seeks to develop in marriage.

Wedding obsessed!

We live in a wedding obsessed culture. A wedding is regarded as not just a social or spiritual event, but the goal of a lifetime. From a young age, girls are trained to dream about their ideal wedding. Many keep scrapbooks detailing the dress, the flowers, the church, the social hall, and the colors. Weddings are regarded as the ultimate status symbol, something to look forward to, plan excessively, and herald in every country throughout the world. Yet one thing often lacking in such lavish weddings is the excitement and preparation for marriage. While upholding weddings, many regard marriage as a drudgery, the ultimate joke. People who are married are often referenced as "trapped." It would appear that as soon as the wedding fun is over, nothing remains of marriage in concept except total boredom, mundanity, and futility.

> **BEHIND THE ARTICLE**
>
> Marriage was one of those topics I avoided discussing in *Power For Today* because I felt there was already so much marriage advice out there, I didn't want to compete with it. The article was an extension of a program I did for an early version of the *Power For Today* radio program where I discussed marriage and the keys to having a marriage that is successful. It was such a popular issue, we re-ran the article in 2013.

While weddings have always been extensive affairs throughout history, the modern disdain for marriage shows in many ways. Due to the frequency of divorce and extremely high rate of unhappy marriages, many have written off marriage as an impossibility all together. Others live in wedding mode permanently, expecting marriage to be a vacation from life. Then there are couples who have been married ten, twenty, even forty or fifty years, and seem, at least on the surface, to have some kind of secret for staying together for so long. Is there such a secret?

The Scriptural approach to marriage

The Scriptures take a different approach to marriage than the world does. While to the world marriage stands as either a social symbol or the ultimate bondage, God's Word reveals both ideal and less-than-ideal circumstances in marriage. One thing quite refreshing about the Scriptures is the full marital spectrum we witness in its pages. We see examples of people who encountered dishonesty in their relationships, marital discord, abuse, abandonment, death, affairs, and happy marriages, displaying the best a relationship has to offer. Rather than giving a fluffy version of marriage that we see in many denominations, the Scriptures are down-to-earth, real, and practical when it comes to marital relationships. While the Word gives us advice on how to have the best possible relationship, it also allows for the reality that not everyone follows that advice.

One of the best words given on the topic of marriage is found at Proverbs 5:18: *Let thy fountain be blessed: and rejoice with the wife of thy youth. Let her be as the loving hind and pleasant roe; let her breasts satisfy thee at all times; and be thou ravished always with her love.* (KJV) These beautiful words give couples the expressed command to enjoy one another. Rather than treat marriage as an institution, these words reveal to us that marriage is personal - it is the person you marry. While the world presents marriage very impersonally - a merging of two individuals, each of which simply fulfill a role the other person has been seeking a mate for their entire lives - the Scriptures display marriage as a person. Passing from an impersonal revelation of marriage to a personal one gives us the ability to rejoice with our spouse - to enjoy them fully - and to pass from an immature relationship to a mature one. The Scriptures definitely require, expound, and call forth Christian marriages to be solidly mature and rooted in Christ.

To reach the place where marriage is personal and enjoyable takes perspective both as a couple and as individuals in a relationship. Following these precepts help couples determine the kind of relationship they desire, the reality of their relationship, and the compatibility they have or do not have. For the remainder of this article, we are going to look at some principles to bring a relationship to maturity.

Set realistic expectations

The first part of this article showed the complete unrealistic dynamic many relationships start out having. People are focused on riding off into the

---

KEY VERSE: PROVERBS 5:19

Let thy fountain be blessed: and rejoice with the wife of thy youth. Let her be as the loving hind and pleasant roe; let her breasts satisfy thee at all times; and be thou ravished always with her love. (KJV)

sunset, having the big, grand, expensive wedding, and then living happily ever after. All too often, couples enter into marriage believing this is indeed what marriage is like.

This is not surprising, given society's approach to marriage. From a young age, children are pressured to imagine the qualities they seek in a mate - and eventually pressured to make those facets a reality. While I am all for selecting a mate who reflects good qualities, we are not going to find a mate who is perfect all the time. The Prince Charming notions of relationships causes us to believe that the mate we select will be charming, perfect, and provide for us a fairy tale life. The princess notion we see tells men they need to rescue and lead women, and that if the two simply fulfill their roles to perfection, they will ride off into the fairy tale sunset.

The problem with this theory is that life is not a fairy tale. Marriage takes place in the real world, where there are real people with real problems. Bills need to be paid, mortgages are due, jobs are difficult, children are disobedient, and marriage seldom if ever looks like it does in a Disney movie. If one is looking for a fairy tale, reality can certainly be disappointing!

Just because marriage is not a fairy tale, however, doesn't mean a marriage can't be solid or enjoyable. What it means is that we must pursue realistic expectations in our marriage. We must expect realistic things from our partner, from ourselves, and out of our marriage. Just like reality counters fairy-tale fantasies, the same is true in marriage.

What does it mean to set a realistic expectation? Setting realistic expectations means we take into account the person we are married to as well as who we are and the situations which exist in our lives. It means we accept the fact that our mate is imperfect in many ways, and that we pick our battles for this reason. Most importantly, when we set realistic expectations in our marriage, we choose to let God work things out in our partners, rather than trying to change them ourselves. It is perfectly natural to find flaws or issues within a mate, but we must also recognize that we don't have the power to change whatever may seem problematic.

A realistic view of marriage sees marriage as a part of life rather than an escape from it. When we see marriage in this perspective, it makes married life easier to handle. Every little problem, character flaw, or difficulty is not cataclysmic; they are simply a part of life. In order to get a realistic perspective on your marriage, start considering your married life and yourself as a married person as a part of the whole in your life. While being married isn't the whole of your existence, it is a big part of how you live and the choices you make. It's also important to consider what is best for a marriage rather than always thinking about what is best for oneself.

The Word offers us an important verse that provides us with aid on adapting a realism in our marriage: *...But as for me and my house, we will* *serve the LORD.* (Joshua 24:15) If we are to remain realistic in our marriages, we must serve God in all we do because that will put our priorities straight, help us in our relationship with our mate, and set us on a right course for our marital lives. Our marriages must be set to serve the Lord so we can be representatives of the Kingdom of God which is more of a reality than any of the cares couples experience in this world.

Don't get married because "it's the next thing to do"

Many can recall Charlotte York's resolution to get married by the end of the year on the popular HBO show, *Sex and the City*. She resolved to take full control of her personal life and find a mate. Enter the scene, Dr. Trey MacDougall, the man who seemed to have everything she wanted – he was rich, successful – and most of all, he was available. The show accurately depicts their all-too fast courtship which ended in a run to the altar and a completely disastrous marriage. No matter how hard they tried to make their marriage work, its complications outweighed the blessings of the marriage. As the season draws on, we learn why: Trey married Charlotte because he had reached a certain age, and it was the "thing" to do. We know Charlotte got married to Trey, despite facts to the contrary, because Charlotte realized she was getting older and still single. In essence, both got married for the same reason: because they were reaching a certain point in their lives where being single did not seem to be a social option.

Getting married to someone for no other reason than one feels it's time to be married is quite common. As people seek to put their lives in a certain order before marriage, it isn't at all uncommon to see the years pass by with individuals single into their late 20s and 30s. The societal push for individuals to marry and have children often leaves older singles feeling out of place, purposeless, and like they need to make a change and get married or else.

You can't make marriage work based on desperation. While marriage can be a great blessing, it is impossible to enjoy someone you select because they are available and you think it's time to get married. If we read the Song of Solomon, considered by many to be the most beautiful expression of love ever, we find the following: *You have stolen my heart, my sister, my bride; you have stolen my heart with one glance of your eyes, with one jewel of your necklace. How delightful is your love, my sister, my bride! How much more pleasing is your love than wine, and the fragrance of your perfume than any spice! Your lips drop sweetness as the honeycomb, my bride; milk and honey are under your tongue. he fragrance of your garments is like that of Lebanon.* (Song of Solomon 4:9-11) Notice desperation is not found anywhere in this passage!

Being single doesn't make one any less successful than a married person. If you believe God is calling you to be married, the only way for a marriage to work is to wait for His timing rather than rushing into a relationship. I believe mostly everyone out there desires to feel the loving connection displayed in the Song of Solomon, but we must realize that rushing into a relationship doesn't result in that type of love. Take the time to know the person you seek to marry BEFORE that trip down the aisle.

Allow each other to be individuals

> **AUTHOR'S REFLECTIONS**
>
> One of the reasons I avoided much teaching on marriage in my earlier years of ministry is because I felt the way it was taught had an elitist air to it. It was as if being married was taught to be good and being single was taught to be bad. There are benefits and negatives to both marriage and single life, but realizing that we don't understand the circumstances that come with either singleness or marriage reminded me that to understand both, we need proper teaching about both.

One of the biggest misconceptions about marriage is that two people get married and then they both cease to be who they are. Instead of being individuals, they morph into this strange married creature where the couple has to do everything together, like all the same things, and pursue all the same interests.

While it is definitely important that couples spend time together and enjoy one another's company, there is nothing anywhere which requires married couples to cease being individuals, as well. The greater respect each party of a couple has for the other party's individuality, the better the chance a marriage has at surviving the years, especially as each person grows and changes.

The Song of Solomon 5:16 says: *...This is my beloved, and this is my friend, O daughters of Jerusalem.* A simple saying, but deep in meaning. Couples are not just called to be people who live under the same roof, but beloved and friends to one another. We don't often think of marriage in this context, but it is often the reason why marriages break up: because couples do not feel loved and supported by their mates. Couples need to learn the precept of loving one another and befriending one another for a marriage to last. Both partners in a relationship need to feel like they can talk to their partner; that they can share their joys and fears, ups and downs, concerns and excitements, and do so without judgment or criticism. Couples need to talk and talk often about what is going on in their lives and where they hope to go. It's also important that couples take the time to love one another rather than just assuming the other person knows how they feel. Spoil your partner a little bit! Make their favorite meal, take them out to their favorite restaurant, take them shopping, watch the kids so they can have an afternoon to themselves, go to the movies, go for a walk, do something fun together! Don't reserve love for Valentine's Day or your anniversary; make it a regular part of the relationship you have as a married couple.

Just as in any relationship, for couples to do well together, they need to feel free to pursue interests, hobbies, and dreams that the other partner may not share or may not share in full. Marriage does not mean sameness, it means oneness! So, take that class, go out with your friends every now and then, and follow the life God has for you in all things; never feel that you have to stop living because God has sent you a mate.

Walking in love

One of the basic keys to a successful and enjoyable relationship with your spouse is the principle that you are a Christian just as much in your marriage as you are with others in your life. Sometimes we forget that the relationship between Christ and the church is pictured as a bride and bridegroom - on purpose. Ephesians 5:32-32 reminds us: *For this reason a man will leave his father and mother and be united to his wife, and the two will become one flesh.' This is a profound mystery—but I am talking about Christ and the church.* The love and commitment of Christ and the church is to reflect in husband and wife, and it is for this reason that the New Testament spends so much time speaking on the marital relationship. The way we are to love and interact with one another is supposed to serve as a shadow or type of the great love Christ has for the church and is to point people toward that eternal relationship rather than away from it. If we remember our command to walk in love, be living witnesses of the Gospel in all we do, and love our spouse as we love ourselves, we can effectively and powerfully walk in love as a witness to the world not just that marriage can work, but that living in Christ works, as well.

The world in which we live poses its challenges for married couples; but if a couple can learn to enjoy one another, they can learn the blessings in God's gift of marriage.

Apostle Marino ministering during children's church Wake Forest, North Carolina (December 2013)

16 MY OWN WAY NEVER REALLY MATTERED ANYWAY!
(Volume 11, Number 3 – May/June 2012)

I was once in service with a pastor who spoke how one of his twin boys insisted on running in the kitchen and touching the stove. He would run in the room, tap the stove hard enough to be noticed, and then run out of the kitchen. Every time he would do this, the pastor would quietly say to him, "You better not touch that stove!" Despite his words, the child kept doing the same thing over and over again. Then one day, the stove was hot, and the child got burned. Without hysterics or changing his tone, the pastor said to his son, "I told you not to touch that stove."

Everyone reading this can remember a time when we just had to have something or do something. Someone probably told us we shouldn't do it and gave us the reasons. Maybe what we wanted to do was dangerous, impossible, or unwise. Maybe what we wanted to do was problematic, it would cause trouble, or harm to ourselves or others. No matter what we might have heard or who warned us, we were insistent on doing whatever we wanted to do in our own way.

How many of us can say what we insisted on doing worked for us? Most of us must face the music in this situation, accepting the fact that going our own way did not benefit us in the least. As difficult as it is to admit, going our own way often leads to complications and trouble rather than productivity and joy.

It is often extremely difficult for people to admit they do not know best in the various areas of their lives. Much of our world today defines itself by personal opinions, outside influences (cleverly designed to make us think they are our ideas), and personal concepts. With such an individualized world, we've walked away with only one value: selfishness. People are so self-aware they have come to believe anything is possible if they will only follow their own ideas.

Most Christians acknowledge the world has a problem with selfishness and self-insistence. Most would not argue there is no question of a selfish, self-centered, self-serving world, thinking its way right. Yet many Christians also fail to see these same attitudes and interest in themselves. This strain of self-interest has spread to the church, where Christians use God as the excuse to be selfish instead of becoming selfless. It is almost as if many think God should be grateful that we agree to serve and believe in Him! Many ministers and leaders have developed lifestyles and measures of success that don't align with the Word but reflect selfish attitudes and desires. Then we have those who seem to get everything they want, no matter how detrimental or anti-God it may be and give God the credit for all they have.

> **BEHIND THE ARTICLE**
>
> I was doing some editing for someone who paid me for the work and then went away on a trip. It turned out the trip didn't accomplish what the man wanted it to, and he didn't wind up doing what he wanted. He relayed to me at the end of his experience, however, "But my own way never really mattered, anyhow!" The result from that one line became an entire study on our own willfulness when it comes to the things of God.

It takes a lot of faithful maturity and spiritual life in Christ to take that step back and realize the ways in which we are going may be self-interested, rather than God-interested. God is calling a generation who will stand back and say, "My own way never really mattered anyway!" How do we reach this point?

Worldly wise men

We've all heard the story of the Magi, the men from Persia who came to bring gifts to the child Jesus. What we don't know about the Magi, however, is very relevant to the story. History has coined them "wise men" and "kings from the Orient." While they might have been regarded as men with earthly wisdom or knowledge, the Magi were not kings. The word "magi" indicates a magician, one who divined the future through astrology and practiced magic. Their specialty was astrology, which they noted by charting and watching changes in the stars. The Magi mentioned in Matthew were most likely followers of Zoroastrianism, individuals who followed a religion mixing Jewish, Gnostic, and eastern ideas. They were a semblance of pagans, relying on human wisdom and magic to get what they wanted out of life.

The Magi were not Christians in disguise, they were not kings, and they were not men guided by the wisdom of God. They were people who had made their lives by going their own way and were quite well-skilled at it. It is clear they believed their methods to be right, as they were not just casual magicians; they were experts in their field, skilled and well-versed in what they did. They were so well-versed in their own ways, in fact, that they were called upon by Herod for a most important task.

Matthew 2:1-8 tells of the early stages of the Magi's experience: *Now when Jesus was born in Bethlehem of Judea in the days of Herod the king, behold, wise men [astrologers] from the east came to Jerusalem, asking, Where is He Who has been born King of the Jews? For we have seen His star in the east at its rising and have come to worship Him. When Herod the king heard this, he was disturbed and troubled, and the whole of Jerusalem with him. So he called together all the chief priests and learned men (scribes) of the people and anxiously asked them where the Christ was to be born. They replied to him, In Bethlehem of Judea, for so it is written by the prophet: And you Bethlehem, in the land of Judah, you are not in any way least or insignificant among the chief cities of Judah; for from you shall come a Ruler (Leader) Who will govern and shepherd My people Israel. Then Herod sent for the wise men [astrologers] secretly, and accurately to the last point ascertained from them the time of the appearing of the star [that is, how long the star had made itself visible since its rising in the east]. Then he sent them to Bethlehem, saying, Go and search for the Child carefully and diligently, and when you have found Him, bring me word, that I too may come and worship Him.* (AMPC)

The Magi were practicing their magical arts when they realized an unusual celestial presence. Their motive to come and honor Christ was an ancient practice by which the highest and most relevant religious and

---

KEY VERSE: MATTHEW 2:12

And receiving an answer to their asking, they were divinely instructed and warned in a dream not to go back to Herod; so they departed to their own country by a different way. (AMPC)

political figures paid homage to newborn or enthroned royalty. They were doing things their own way, unaware that God had His own purpose in motivating their desire to honor Christ. Even though Herod's desire was less than honorable (he was concerned about a threat to his power), Herod knew these Magi were the people to find the child Jesus.

Home via another route

Matthew 2:9-12 finishes the story of the Magi's visit to Christ: *When they had listened to the king, they went their way, and behold, the star which had been seen in the east in its rising went before them until it came and stood over the place where the young Child was. When they saw the star, they were thrilled with ecstatic joy. And on going into the house, they saw the Child with Mary His mother, and they fell down and worshiped Him. Then opening their treasure bags, they presented to Him gifts--gold and frankincense and myrrh. And receiving an answer to their asking, they were divinely instructed and warned in a dream not to go back to Herod; so they departed to their own country by a different way.* (AMPC) The recounting of the Magi's experience specifically states they went on their own way to find Christ. How many of us do this same thing? We are set and determined to find Christ our own way and by our own methods. We have our own goal in mind...and yet God has another purpose all together! Such was with the Magi: they had their own way but experienced something profound in their experience with Christ. So profound, in fact, that God moved them to go home by a different way. They were told by God, **DO NOT GO YOUR OWN WAY!** Returning by their own way would have consequences for Christ's life and their own lives. These men, not knowing the true God, knew something beyond their magical ways gave them a divine guidance...and they obeyed.

What amazes me most is the vast number of people who don't take a hint that even magic men could decode. Many in the church today insist on their own way, leading to the world and ultimately, spiritual or physical death. In self-insistent stubbornness, many remain adamant that their way is best, and they will follow their way, even if consequences result. But if the magic men of Persia could hear from God and, in humility, obey, so much more should Christians respond positively to following God's way!

A self-interested church

Many abhorrent doctrines emerging over the past 200 years have crept into the church, causing a rush of selfish believers. Instead of recognizing themselves as selfish, they blame their fleshly indulgences on God's blessing. Such concepts have caused faith to be all about the believer and

Jesus, ignoring the church body of believers and outside impact. More and more I note the incredibly self-centered faith many seem to have. Discussion is all about what God is doing for or in them, not about what they should do now that God has done all this for them. The measure of faith comes in the form of material goods rather than in spiritual growth or faith. In other words, most of the church lives by the precept, "He who has the most toys, wins."

Anyone versed in the Word of God knows we can't measure our faith lives by our material successes. While God does provide for His faithful people, wicked people can achieve material success by following worldly ways. How much "stuff" we have doesn't give any indication of the awesomeness of God in our lives! What does reflect God is the impact we have on others, and that impact is measured by the fruit our lives are bearing. How do we defy such self-interest? We learn exactly what God intends for us to learn in the Spiritual life.

Isaiah 30:18-21 delivers a powerful message of responsibility to New Covenant believers: *And therefore will the LORD wait, that He may be gracious unto you, and therefore will He be exalted, that He may have mercy upon you: for the LORD is a God of judgment: blessed are all they that wait for Him. For the people shall dwell in Zion at Jerusalem: thou shalt weep no more: He will be very gracious unto thee at the voice of thy cry; when He shall hear it, He will answer thee. And though the Lord give you the bread of adversity, and the water of affliction, yet shall not thy teachers be removed into a corner any more, but thine eyes shall see thy teachers: And thine ears shall hear a word behind thee, saying, This is the way, walk ye in it, when ye turn to the right hand, and when ye turn to the left.* (KJV) New Covenant believers have no excuse, because God's teaching has been made known to us! Are there false teachers? Sure, there is no question about that. Yet despite false teachers, God has appointed His teachers to herald His message and make it so clear and so known that there is nowhere which we can go without knowing His way. We have no excuse to say we don't know God's way because He has revealed it unto us. Thus the answer to combating selfishness, self-centeredness, and self-interest is to obey the ways of God and follow God's ways instead of our own!

How do we measure where we are?

Measuring faith by things or worldly progress has caused great jealousy in the church as well. If we measure our relationship with God by what we have, it is only a matter of time before Christian relationships become competitive. How does competition start? For no other reason than believing faith is all about us and making our way possible. When we do not sacrifice our way for God's way, things become about nothing more than getting what we want. Many people seem to be moving on, but where they are moving to has no relevance. They may be in a new location, in a new church, or doing a new thing, but they still have all the same problems, spiritual issues, superficiality, and selfishness. The more they insist on moving on, the more it seems like they get what they want. Thinking that God is behind such lack of progress is in error.

Such "spinning" is not new. The Israelites "spun" themselves in circles for forty years, seeming to move on and make progress, but in reality, they were not going anywhere: *The Israelites had moved about in the desert forty years until all the men who were of military age when they left Egypt had died, since they had not obeyed the LORD. For the LORD had sworn to them that they would not see the land that He had solemnly promised their fathers to give us, a land flowing with milk and honey.* (Joshua 5:6) Just because you are moving fast doesn't mean you are going somewhere! The way to measure our success in where we are does not lie in how fast we are going, but in how well we are adhering to the ways of God in everything. God's way often does not mirror what we might expect, and it may mean waiting to move on or moving in a totally different direction than we might like to go.

> **AUTHOR'S REFLECTIONS**
>
> Admitting that we are willful and disobedient as people is never an easy process, but it is essential we break the denial off ourselves and assess ourselves properly. If we are disobedient, we are not ever going to see ourselves go or move anywhere by the Spirit.

Turning around and going God's way

The very heart of conversion is stopping what we're doing and turning around, following God's way instead of our own. Mark 1:4-5 says: *John the Baptist appeared in the wilderness (desert), preaching a baptism [obligating] repentance (a change of one's mind for the better, heartily amending one's ways, with abhorrence of his past sins) in order to obtain forgiveness of and release from sins. And there kept going out to him [continuously] all the country of Judea and all the inhabitants of Jerusalem; and they were baptized by him in the river Jordan, as they were confessing their sins.* (AMPC) In conversion (signified through our water baptism) we die to our old life and stubborn ways and rise again unto God's new life, beginning again and heading on His pathway. No longer are we to seek our own insistence; we have died to the flesh that seeks only itself.

What direction are you heading in? Whose ways do you follow? Conversion doesn't mean we keep insisting God should do things the way we want or give us what we want all the time. If we have truly converted to the Lord, we accept His ways as right, true, and leading us to life. We can live the "religious" way and seemingly do everything that appears right, but this is just as much following our own way as selfish insistence is. God is not looking for people that follow traditions or nice ideas, but people that truly commit themselves to listening to His teachers and discovering His way that leads to life.

It's time for those who claim to be God's people to stop wandering around in the desert after their own concepts and ideas and truly move into His land of promise for them. It is time for God's true people to stand up, putting Him first in all things. No longer should people calling themselves Christians put themselves first and argue with God over principle. We must love God and our neighbor. We must make the ways of God known instead of hiding them and raising up religious ideas. We must stand up and be counted for the Lord. Those who follow God's way aren't ashamed to speak the words, "We are His people, and He is our God!"

The story I opened this article with reflects the immaturity of a person who can't accept advice, wisdom, or foresight. In lacking these essential aspects of maturity, they insist on having their own way at any cost. As God's people, we cannot say we love God and insist on following our own way. If Persian magicians can see the relevance in following divine advice, we too can see it as a great treasure and follow it to the end. Today more than ever before, God is seeking a people who will say, "MY OWN WAY NEVER REALLY MATTERED ANYWAY!"

Apostle Marino ministering during children's church at Sanctuary International Fellowship Tabernacle – SIFT in Raleigh, North Carolina (June 2016)

17 HOLINESS
(Volume 12, Number 1 – January/February 2014)

When I was first a Christian, I never heard much about holiness. My concept of the "holy" was that it was a week prior to Easter set aside for us to go to church a lot. In the Catholic Church, we would say something was "holy" when it was blessed by a priest for a special purpose. Other than that, the only thing "holy" seemed to be the Holy Spirit! Understanding ourselves as holy was not something emphasized, and it continued to be a lesser point of emphasis in the first church I attended after conversion. I heard about how God wanted me to prosper and be healed. I heard that God wanted me to have an awesome life. I heard that God had a future for me. I never, ever heard about holiness. I thought holiness was a religious movement from the 1800s that died out a long time ago. Even many of the holiness churches, such as the Methodist denomination, have moved away from their holiness roots.

When I became an apostolic in 2002, discussion of holiness was more common, but we were never quite told what it was. Holiness was, among those to whom I belonged, a long list of "dont's" that often revolved around the external: don't cut your hair. Don't wear pants if you are a woman. Don't wear short-sleeved shirts if you are a man. Don't ever wear shorts. Don't wear make-up if you are a woman. This list of arbitrary rules gave the impression that holiness was all about stuff we do to ourselves rather than about who we are from the inside out, transformed and redeemed by Christ.

The examples above show the extreme confusion the average Christian has about the call to holiness. Not properly understanding it leads to extremes: those who try too hard to walk in it, they stumble into legalism, while others who don't care enough to attend to it wind up away from it all together.

Even though Christians are vastly confused, holiness is making a comeback in some circles today: not in hair, shorts, shirts, make-up and pants, but in the hearts of those who seek God rightly: *And ye shall be holy unto Me: for I the Lord am holy, and have severed you from other people, that ye should be Mine.* (Leviticus 20:26, KJV)

> **BEHIND THE ARTICLE**
>
> Even though I love all editions of *Power For Today* Magazine, I do have my favorites. This edition and this article are definitely in my top five of favorite editions and articles ever published in our magazine. Written in response to a question about holiness and what it was, this article helped explain the principle of holiness in a modern context.

What is holiness?

"Holy" is a word thrown around in a number of different contexts. To properly understand holiness, we need to first understand that holiness is not limited to a certain denomination, way of thinking, or items somehow blessed or made special by someone of a certain religious standing. Understanding this will help us to see holiness for what it really is. Even though some belief systems attempt to make holiness really complicated, the word "holy" simply means "set apart." When someone or something is "holy," that means it has been set apart for the service, work, and purposes of God. Holiness does not require absurd behavior, but it does require different behavior. If something or someone is being set apart, that means it is taken from something else and now exclusively purposed in a different way. This helps us to understand our role as holy people: believers in Christ are set apart from the world, being taken away from ungodly things and ungodly influences, and set apart as examples of repentance, love, and the standards of God in this world.

Throughout the ages the world has tried to reduce holiness to sets of guidelines and principles that will make holiness externally noticeable. The problem with this is that it is easy for people to follow rules, but often very difficult to stand in integrity when the rules falter or gaps exist in these systems. We also begin to see abuses of power as people try to intervene on God's behalf and start to define holiness by their own personal standards rather than by God's Word. If being holy means simply being set apart - or different - how can we, as believers, understand how it manifests in our lives?

God: the standard of holiness

The book of Leviticus contains extensive codes, regulations, and rules about the Old Testament offerings, hygiene codes, and principles of "separateness." While Leviticus is seldom studied in depth today, it contains for us a great wealth of insight into what it means to be holy. Even though the way in which we approach God is different today, Leviticus provides for us the image of holiness in a way we can understand the separateness God asks of us.

God was - and is - separate from all other gods. In the ancient world, a myriad of different deities surrounded the Israelites as the pagan nations around them sought out the various gods for this, that, or something else. The fact that Jehovah God, the one true God, was one God - separate and unique from all the rest - separated Him from the various pantheons and dualities that plagued ancient belief. This provides us with an excellent image of "separateness" in holiness. God Himself stood out because He was different from these other deities.

As a result of being different, not just anyone can come just any which way before God. The uniqueness, separateness, and specialness of our God means that everything is not acceptable before Him. As a result, the Hebrews had long and extensive guidelines about how to go before God, what was considered acceptable, what was clean or unclean, and how to appropriately respond and behave in the presence of an all-holy, all magnificent God.

Despite the extensive guidelines about that which was clean and unclean, and acceptable and unacceptable, we see that God commanded His people to bring forth offerings out of common, everyday items. Even though God was holy, set apart, and different, He was still approachable enough to accept things that were common to everyday living.

KEY VERSE: 1 PETER 2:9-10

But ye are a chosen generation, a royal priesthood, an holy nation, a peculiar people; that ye should shew forth the praises of Him Who hath called you out of darkness into His marvellous light; which in time past were not a people, but are now the people of God: which had not obtained mercy, but now have obtained mercy. (KJV)

This tells us three very key things about holiness. The first is that holiness means being different - set apart - from something else. In our circumstance, it means that we are separate or set apart from the world. This brings us to the second thing: Even though we are set apart, we must still be approachable. Being holy doesn't mean we retreat so far away from the world that nobody can relate to us anymore. It simply means that when we are approached, we must be approached correctly, upholding certain standards of decency and order. When people come to us, we may give a certain allowance of time for them to understand that we do not disrespect ourselves or others around us, but we excel with a spirit of excellence. The third thing it tells us is that even though we are a holy and set apart people, we are not called to be arrogant or haughty. We are around common, ordinary items and God has created us to be ordinary people living among other ordinary people in this world. As we are holy, God births extraordinary qualities in us and we remain grounded by the ordinary, everyday things and lives we live. In holiness, we do not stop living. We are not mandated to stop watching television, listening to music, visiting with family or friends, or stop dressing like normal people. It simply means we are called to be more selective about what we allow into our lives and more conscious about how those things reflect around us.

In the world, but not of the world

The common, everyday items God commanded the Hebrews to use for sacrificial offerings were things in this world - but they were suddenly called to be used for a higher purpose, for something that was above this world. Those objects of the ancient sacrifices teach us something powerful about ourselves and our call to holiness in this world. In John 17:14-18, Jesus prays the following for His disciples: *I have given them Thy Word; and the world hath hated them, because they are not of the world, even as I am not of the world. I pray not that Thou shouldest take them out of the world, but that Thou shouldest keep them from the evil. They are not of the world, even as I am not of the world. Sanctify them through Thy truth: Thy Word is truth. As Thou hast sent me into the world, even so have I also sent them into the world.* (KJV) In other words, Jesus was praying for His disciples to be holy. Just like the ordinary things used in sacrifice did not cease from common usage but were used for a transforming purpose, so too we are called to remain in this world, around common things and working in ordinary purposes. As human beings, we still have to work jobs, pay bills, go to the grocery store, and maintain our lives, just like other people. We still deal with difficult people, life struggles, and experience victories and losses. We don't stop living in this world because we have been set apart and holy. The difference within us is now that we are holy, we are simply not of this world anymore. Our priorities, aspirations, purposes, and desires are no longer to look the same as the world's. As we remain in the world but not of it, we reflect a principle of excellence in everything we do.

When being in the world causes us to be different

If we are in this world but not of this world, that means Jesus has caused us to remain here for His purposes. In a practical sense, walking in and reflecting excellence should be something that sets us apart. Even though we are ordinary in this world, we should seek to excel for an extraordinary purpose. This doesn't mean everyone in the Kingdom should aspire to be a television preacher or the CEO of a Fortune 500 company. What it does mean is this: every day, in every possible way, we should be striving to do the best possible job and live the best possible life, all according to the precepts God has laid out for us in His Word. Being excellent doesn't mean being an overachiever, it simply means representing and doing the best possible job we can in any situation.

If we step back and think about it, every one of us has the ability to be excellent, every single day. Whether it's doing a great job for our employer, dressing in a way that reflects grace and self-respect, handling our families with purpose and honor, being excellent stewards with the resources we have, or simply being someone who is able to reach out, encourage, and embrace other people, being a person of excellence is an important mark of holiness. We serve an excellent God, Who has, in all things, given us the best He has throughout history. In our own situations, God has given us the best throughout our relationship with Him. It is our honor - and our privilege - to be His people, reflecting His excellence in our holiness.

The Prophet Daniel was a true example of excellence in holiness. When faced with defiling himself with the king's food and bowing to a false god, Daniel made a stand against such things. He trusted God enough to fast while others were feasting and stand for God's truth, even in the face of being thrown in a furnace. His reputation went before him, as was evident in King Belshazzar's statements: *Then was Daniel brought in before the king. And the king spake and said unto Daniel, Art thou that Daniel, which art of the children of the captivity of Judah, whom the king my father brought out of Jewry? I have even heard of thee, that the spirit of the gods is in thee, and that light and understanding and excellent wisdom is found in thee.* (Daniel 5:13-14, KJV). The excellent spirit of God was able to manifest in Daniel's excellence, because Daniel was willing to set himself apart for God's service. Daniel, in other words, was willing to be holy!

Being different

We can talk all day long about holiness, but our willingness to be different for the Lord really does come down to our choices. Too often today we see people who claim to be Christians, and yet they resemble the patterns and behaviors of the world. Despite their claims, they dress, act, and pursue the aspirations, interests, and desires of those people who have not been sanctified. This is truly not the way that those who are in the world, but not of the world, should be. There should just be something different about a Christian. While yes, we still have to do the things other people to do to survive, those things should not be our common focus and life aspirations. When people see our excellence, that excellence pointes them unto the One Who is truly excellent in each and every possible way.

I think being different frightens people. The idea of having to stand out, behave differently, and be removed from the crowd intimidates many. It does not, however, change the Christian's command to be different. We have been left here in this world to make a difference with our difference! 1 Peter 2:9-10 says: *But ye are a chosen generation, a royal priesthood, an holy nation, a peculiar people; that ye should shew forth the praises of Him Who hath called you out of darkness into His marvellous light; Which in time past were not a people, but are now the people of God: which had not obtained mercy, but now have obtained mercy."* (KJV) The very reason we can be holy - to be different - to be peculiar - to be called into light - is all thanks to the great and wonderful mercy of God. That mercy has transformed us into a people who are able to bring about this difference to the world. That means that even though being different may be uncomfortable at times, may cause our relationships with others to change,

> **AUTHOR'S REFLECTIONS**
>
> We talk so much about being set apart, royal, chosen, holy, and different that I don't think we understand just how difficult it is to adopt such principles in our lives. Recently we had a woman leave our church because as much as she wanted to be different and genuinely wanted to step out into the realm of being peculiar, she wound up being more comfortable in the old ways of church life that revolved around gossip, fitting in, and in teaching she was more familiar with. Tradition will leave us thinking we are more advanced in God than we are, and even though she started out with a great attitude, the challenges of being different were not ones she was comfortable with as time went on. Being different is difficult! Never forget this in your walk with Him. If you are finding what you are called to do to be too easy, then you are probably not hearing from God.

and may mean that we do things differently from other people, the mercy of God has given us the grace and ability to go forward in our different state. We've been endowed with courage, purpose, and sound thinking to represent the difference God has worked in our lives.

Holiness beyond rules

There will be more times than not in your Christian journey where you are confronted with situations that don't have a general "rule" to follow in order to solve the dilemma or choice at hand. It needs to mean something to us that God has called us a "holy nation, a peculiar people." If these things identify us, that means they transcend a long list of rules by which we conduct ourselves. The Bible speaks of the promise of people who would have God's Word written on their hearts and would obey God simply because they love Him. In holiness, we find the perfect purpose to godly obedience. He has set us apart, made us different, given us a new perspective and a perpetual pursuit of excellence, and all of this manifests that we might obey Him in all things. 2 Corinthians 3:2-3 says, *Ye are our epistle written in our hearts, known and read of all men: Forasmuch as ye are manifestly declared to be the epistle of Christ ministered by us, written not with ink, but with the Spirit of the living God; not in tables of stone, but in fleshy tables of the heart.* (KJV) The bottom line of holiness is that we are people who seek to obey God, that we might glorify Him in all we do. Even though the rules of man were established to help create guidelines, they do not come close to helping us become a people who are holy, listening to the commands of God as are written on our heart. In every situation, God is speaking to us via His inward witness, the Spirit guiding us into all truth. It is our command, our purpose to learn to hear Him speak to us, that we might fulfill His will in the earth.

Being holy is a process. It starts as we understand God's Word to us in the context of our lives today and extends out as we make more and more changes to accept and receive His guidance and direction throughout our lives. The holier we become, the more set apart we also become, exclusively purposed for God and His service. His witness transforms us in this life from mere common, ordinary people to something extraordinary: a holy nation created and brought forth to let the world know He is real and He has an awesome and amazing purpose for every person on this earth.

Apostle Marino introducing one of her books in Daytona Beach, Florida (August 2014)

18 HOLDING ONTO HOPE IN THE MIDST OF HOPELESSNESS
(Volume 9, Number 3—March 2010)

Once I went to a church where a minister stood up and spoke for over an hour about the young adult group he belonged to which introduced him to Jesus Christ. He spoke of how perfect he thought the members of the group were, how he really believed that these were people who lived a perfect Christian life. Within a few months of joining this group, this particular man was in for a shock. One member of the group went to rehab for drug use. Two other members backslid into sin and left the group and Christianity all together. One girl announced she was six months pregnant, and hiding her pregnancy under baggy clothes. When all this happened, he became totally disillusioned by the events around him. What was most amazing, however, was that, according to his recounts of this story and others which he tied in, this minister, to this very day, experienced doubt as a Christian as a result of these events. He now experiences hopelessness every time someone comes to him with a problem. To hear him deliver his message was almost like listening to an AA testimony. You could still hear the hopelessness elicited all these years later by new circumstances that remind him of that early circumstance. Apparently, over twenty years later, he is still carrying around a hopelessness that hasn't been resolved.

Another individual I worked with was a little bit bolder in speaking of his disillusionment. He couldn't figure out why becoming a Christian wasn't this big "before and after" experience. To hear him tell his story, here it is, all these years later, and God still hasn't met with his perceived expectations. He didn't wake up smarter or more enlightened or profoundly directed with a calling. He never received the Gifts of the Spirit, which he believed to be at the fault of God. And now, he's not only hopeless, but he's also angry, profoundly angry at God because he feels God somehow failed him. His anger manifests in his negative attitude toward tithing and giving, a total unwillingness to conform in obedience to God's will, and in general jealousy and anger toward those who receive from God what he seeks from Him. Such an attitude has caused him to venture into spiritually dangerous areas, voids, and despair.

> **BEHIND THE ARTICLE**
>
> I wrote this particular article during a very challenging and hopeless period in my own life, knowing that if I did some research on hopelessness in Scripture, it would help me to gain my own needed perspective and balance in my life.

There are vast numbers of Christians who feel depressed, lonely, angry, and lost, all with the commonality of feeling hopeless. Underlying their various expressions of thought and feeling lie a life without purpose, meaning, and hope. I don't make light of the hopelessness that people feel whether it's the housewife with postpartum, the elderly man who is sick and alone, or the person who just feels like they're missing something in life. I know I've spent many times feeling hopeless in my life because I just had no idea how anything could ever get better than it was at that moment. Yet I know that at the hopeless points in my life, and at those others reach, too, that we always forget something, or should I say some One, who can help us through, and maybe even eventually understand.

We forget God.

Settling Christian myths

There's a popular myth circling around today that being a Christian will magically cause all our problems to vanish. All we must do is make a little walk to the altar to sign a card and then everything negative or problematic in our lives will vanish. In our fervor of having the perfect life and our disillusionment over falling short of the problem-less existence we seek, we often find life falling short of our expectations. In our discouragement, we fail to look to God, as we should.

Thus, God becomes the last place we seek for our answers rather than the first. I remember going through a time in my life where I was so hopeless and disillusioned that I was just plain out of ideas, and I finally called out to God in one of those "I have no idea God!" moments. Then, I realized: God, the Creator, the first before there was anything else, was the last place I was seeking out. Suddenly this sounded backward, and I wondered if perhaps my feelings of despair and hopelessness were being worsened and not bettered by that fact. Instead of trusting God to help lead me out of my situation, I was leaning on what I thought was best, causing myself stress and turmoil in the process. I was making my own hopelessness more intense and more troublesome!

<u>*Where there is no storm*</u>

The day after I had the realization that leaning on what I might think is best is not beneficial to my spiritual and mental state, God brought me to the Odes of Solomon 32:4 which revealed a powerful truth to me: *Deep in the illuminated mind is no storm.*[1] I thought about this verse over and over again, because it reveals something to us about our turmoil. The passage doesn't say that there is NO STORM, it simply says that in the illuminated mind there is no storm. The verse doesn't promise to remove the storms from our life. In the mind illuminated by God's life, light, and truth, there is no storm. Despite what may rage around us, we have Jesus, the Light of the world, illuminating our hearts and minds so we may find hope, despite whatever we are going through. It is illuminated as we grow deep in our faith and live changed, transformed, and lightened by truth.

Christians are called to be a changed and transformed people, paralleling growth in our faith. Too often we get stuck somewhere, waiting for things to change instead of living in a constant sense of God's hope. We claim that we'll change and find hope when hope comes knocking at our door...but isn't that the opposite of what we should be doing? We should be living in the blessing of NO STORM in the MIDST of A STORM! Waiting for the storm to pass and claim hope lies at the end is nonsense. We can live in the benefit of hope and find hope no matter how hopeless we may be feeling!

So where is the hope? It lies in knowing why we feel so hopeless. As we begin to discover what we are looking toward and why, we can look to God and grow into the fullness of hope He has for us to dwell therein.

> **KEY VERSE: PSALM 37:7**
>
> Be still before the LORD and wait patiently for Him; do not fret when men succeed in their ways, when they carry out their wicked schemes.

Our problems haven't disappeared

Many of us become Christians under the same guise as those I mentioned at the beginning of this article. There is a big push for God to make everything in our lives right, even if things have been wrong for a very long time. We expect to become perfect people overnight, magically transformed into perfection. Any trace of our former life imperfections should magically disappear before our very eyes…and we get angry, discouraged, downhearted, and sour when this does not happen. Erase the notion that being a Christian fixes every problem you've ever had, because it doesn't. Don't expect Jesus to magically come in your life and wave a magic wand over years of debt, bad marriages, bad relationships, life difficulties, addictions, failures, or problems with your job. Jesus definitely heals us everywhere we hurt but the methods by which He heals us don't always undo the negative aftereffects of the deeds we've sown. If you want better results, make better choices. Don't blame your problems on being a Christian! Many of you had those problems before you ever heard about Jesus or being a Christian. Be fair. It took you years to get in your problems, give God at least that many years to help you get out! God is working even if things don't seem to be where we would like them to be. Much of the Christian life is spent waiting on God, trusting in Him to work things out even when we don't see a way for that to happen. Repeatedly we see the command to wait on God throughout the Word, despite circumstances, experiences, or issues which may prompt us to zoom past God. Psalm 37:7 gives us words of inspiration on this matter: *Be still before the LORD and wait patiently for Him; do not fret when men succeed in their ways, when they carry out their wicked schemes.* As long as we live this side of heaven and Jesus has not yet returned, we will have troubles. In the face of such despair, we wait patiently and stand in hope.

The world discourages us

The earthquake in Haiti. The wars in Iraq and Afghanistan. Hurricanes Rita and Katrina. Severe snowstorms in China. Then there are the disasters of another kind: spiritual unrest, emotional disruption and disorders, poverty, addiction, and abuse, as only a sample of issues present in the world today. The state of the world seems to be constantly changing around us, always reminding us of how serious and intense the problems of the world have become. I've heard my mother often say she never thought she would live to see the day that some things that are coming to pass would. While I do not believe it is harder to be a Christian today than it has ever been, many things exist today that pose a challenge to the Christian walk and life. Even being a Christian can pose a certain level of observant discouragement when we review situations through a Christian spirit. The despair and problems of the world can cause us to feel badly, knowing our times befall issues we can't solve, no matter how many times we extend ourselves in faith to try and make a difference. We must remain strong in our faith, and focused in our spiritual discipline. Problems become insurmountable every time we take our eyes off Jesus and put our focus on our problems instead. During these times, we must always remember our calling as Christians and Jesus' words in John 16:33: *These things I have spoken unto you, that ye might have peace. In the world ye shall have tribulation: but be of good cheer; I have overcome the world.* (KJV) Jesus doesn't promise we won't have problems or that the tribulations of the world will cease; but that He has overcome the world, and therefore, we can be at peace and of good cheer. What an awesome prospect! In the midst of worldly hopelessness and despair, we can have hope! It doesn't matter how bad things look because we've read the end of the book, we know the promises that lie ahead, and we know what happens to those who trust in God instead of trusting in the world. We must commit to be a people who trust in God and not the circumstances we see in the world around us.

We don't understand life and the meaning of life

Too many people, Christians included, think life is inherently meaningful simply because it's life. If this indeed was true, we would have no need for callings or even Jesus because life wouldn't require that we seek salvation from death. If life was inherently meaningful, we wouldn't have to make any choices in our life, and most of all, no matter what we would choose to do, it would always be right and therefore we would never combat depression or hopelessness. Life has meaning when we follow God's will for our lives, and that happens because we choose to follow God's will. People who sit around and wait for the meaning of life to fall on their heads never find it. Living in a discouraging world, we must always remember Jesus' promise in John 10:10: *The thief comes only in order to steal and kill and destroy. I came that they may have and enjoy life, and have it in abundance (to the full, till it overflows).* (AMPC) Seeking the meaning of life in life itself will leave you severely void of hope. What we must do instead is seek the Lord as to how our lives can have greater meaning. While meaning doesn't lie in life itself, that doesn't mean we can't find the true meaning of life and the true purpose in life itself. It just means we have to put forth the effort to follow God and make our lives meaningful through obedience to Him.

We've started something that's not of God, made a mess, and now expect God to fix it

> **AUTHOR'S REFLECTIONS**
>
> It's an awful feeling to feel swallowed up by life. Unfortunately, many Christians feel this way because they haven't been taught that God is not just there for our optimism, but for every situation and feeling that we might encounter in our lives. Learning to rely on Him makes a monumental difference in our war on hopelessness, despair, and depression.

Abraham, Sarah, Hagar, and Ishmael. David, Bathsheba, and their first child. The Hebrews and wanting a King. Ananias, Sapphira, and their withheld offering. The Scriptures are full of people who got a bright idea as a way to "help out God" on the way to what they want and totally went out of God's will for them in the meantime. Then they get in a severe bind for their troubles and want God to come along and fix everything and when God says, "I didn't make this mess, fix it yourself," Who gets the blame? God. This isn't fair. God has made every possible prevision and opportunity for us to experience blessing and grace beyond measure in our lives. When we go out of our way to go out of God's way, the responsibility for that mess goes to none but ourselves. Hebrews 12:2 says that Jesus is *the author and finisher of our faith*, but Jesus isn't obliged to finish anything He didn't start! The first thing we have to do in this situation is repent – not blame God – for our mess. Then we must seek God for how to make the situation right, and get back on the right track. God will lead us to where we need to be when we turn to Him in humility. Pride will only get us further and further away from His will, and more and more into trouble. If you have created a situation out of God's will, it's time to return to the basics of repentance: turn around and change your ways, and begin going in God's way instead of your own.

Hopeless circumstances exist, but hopelessness is optional

Part of being a solid, stable, mature Christian means we follow what God has for us to do as best we can, remembering His promises and precepts to us. Hopeless circumstances are a part of living in an unsaved world, but hopelessness is optional. And although most Christians will encounter hopelessness at one point in their life or another, the reality is that we don't have to stay that way, letting the world defeat us. Instead of looking to God as our last resort, we need to seek Him out as our first resort, as this is a sign of our faith and trust in Him.

The resurrection of Jesus Christ proves to every single one of us that hope exists, no matter how bleak a circumstance may be. Jesus overcame the very power of death itself, defying it in one single action. Even though many have reduced Christianity to nothing more than financial gain and easy living, Christianity is based in an overcoming Spirit, leading us to eternal life and victory. We can't be overcomers if we never overcome anything, and we can't overcome if we sit in a place of hopeless discouragement. We need to set ourselves not to look at circumstances, no matter how insurmountable they may seem. We must become more than just individuals who hope for the best; we must seek to be the best we can be in Christ Jesus. As we stand lighted in our minds with the light of God's Son, Jesus Christ, Jesus, the Son of God then becomes our focus. We will rise again and not fear, no matter what is going on. If it means turning off the television, radio, and internet, so be it; we are going to be a people that have hope, offer hope, and stand as symbols of hope in a troublesome and dying world. In a world that never has the answers, we are going to offer a true answer to problems through our countenance, demeanor, and life of faith.

I am sure that the cross and overcoming death seemed insurmountable on that final Friday. Death seemed to reign supreme, and Satan seemed to have the upper hand, as far as the surface eye could see. The good news for Jesus, on that day, and for us in every hopeless circumstance remains: the resurrection is only a Sunday away.

---

[1] *The Odes of Solomon* as found in *The Other Bible*, edited by Willis Barnstone. San Francisco, California: Harper Collins San Francisco, 1984.

Apostle Marino teaching a Bible Study at Sanctuary Apostolic Fellowship (to become Sanctuary International Fellowship Tabernacle – SIFT) in Raleigh, North Carolina (October 2015)

The Seven Churches of Revelation, Part 1
(Volume 13, Number 3 – Third Quarter 2015)

Have you read the book of Revelation or heard teaching on it? If you have been in church in the past thirty years, odds are good you have encountered at least one series of teaching on the book of Revelation. Usually Sci-Fi and futuristic in interpretation, study on the book of Revelation tends to take on a dramatic characteristic, something that wows people as the book of Revelation becomes the *Star Wars* of the church. Exploding fires, asteroids hitting earth, intimidating political forces, people being forced to do certain things and take certain marks - all of it makes for a great and mighty story, something that sounds like an eternal drama playing out, a final hurrah to round out human experience.

It sounds good…it sounds intriguing and interesting…but is this why the book of Revelation was written? Was the whole purpose of Revelation to provide good literary fodder to finish the Bible? Does it exist so we can write fictional books and speculate what will happen in between its contents? Is Revelation there for our entertainment, T-shirts, and to be the endless cause of debate for centuries?

The answer to these questions, answered in one sentence is no,

Revelation was not penned to be a dramatic fodder to entertain us. In fact, Revelation has been a controversial book for centuries, one that was included in the Bible and then excluded and was not highly regarded by most of the Reformers, nor by the Orthodox Church as a denomination. The reason for such controversy over its contents, I believe, is the way we have interpreted it and the way in which we turn Revelation into something that is clearly for our amusement rather than something that is there to teach us something important.

The proof that Revelation was never meant to be a long-winded drama (not unlike some of the preachers who teach on it) is found in the second and third chapters of Revelation, where Jesus talks about something many might find boring or mundane: he has the Apostle John write seven letters, one to each of seven churches located in Asia. They aren't fancy, they aren't written to be eloquent, but they were written to pay attention to and call discipline and praise where it was needed. The things that might have been minor to some other onlookers were noticed by God, and in turn, they were addressed in these letters.

> **BEHIND THE ARTICLE**
>
> When I wrote my book, *All That Is Seen And Unseen: A Journey Through The Book Of Revelation*, the thing that stood out most to me was the seven churches of Revelation. I was so taken with them and felt that the revelation contained within them was so vital, we needed to do a feature on them in *Power For Today* Magazine.

Why Revelation Was Written To The Church

The thing most people miss in the book of Revelation is the fact that it was written to the church, not the world. People are quick to use the writings of Revelation to try and pin things on the world (especially to plug in prophetic headlines), but Revelation does not exist for this purpose. I like to call the book of Revelation the "Daniel of the New Testament." What this means is that the book of Revelation exists to include the church as a part of prophetic history and, in some ways, as a central part of prophetic history. Just as Daniel chronicles the happenings of the temple and the rise and fall of nations within the book's pages, so Revelation shows that the history of the church is a part of that history. It is a part of prophecy, it is a part of the world, and it is a part of the past, present, and future of the spiritual realm.

This means the seven churches that were addressed in the beginning of Revelation were not addressed by accident. It wasn't something just stuck in there to make the book seem doctrinal. If Revelation exists to prove the church is a part of prophecy, that means everything the church does matters to God. There is nothing far from His sight, nor nothing distant from Him.

The church needs to know its identity, and the seven churches of Revelation prove this to us. Rather than viewing them as different historical eras of church history, the seven churches of Revelation ARE the church. Every one of us has been to a church with some of the issues represented by those seven churches. Most likely, we have been a part of churches that combine different aspects of all seven of these churches under one roof. Developing in different places with different circumstances and needs, the issues these seven churches had reveal much to us about what is going on in the church, what we need to address as a church, and the things we need to look at first before we ever start pointing fingers at others.

Revelation isn't all about the future. Even though the book of Revelation is spoken of most of the time in a futuristic context, Revelation is about all of time: the church past, present, and future. Much of what is revealed in Revelation exists right now, in the spiritual realm, and through the book of Revelation, we are privileged to see it in action. The seven churches: Ephesus, Smyrna, Pergamum, Thyatira, Sardis, Philadelphia and Laodicea have much to offer us and tell us much about ourselves. It is a part of looking at the church now as much as the church later. In this two-part study, we will be looking at just that: and how viewing these foundational chapters in context changes our entire perspective on the book of Revelation.

The Apostle John and the Churches

On an important note for the modern readers: there is nothing that indicates the Apostle John directly covered any of the seven churches in Revelation, save the one at Pergamum, where he installed a bishop. If anything, we see a very different side of the apostolic than we are used to in the modern church. While space does not allow me to get into a long detail about the significance of the Apostle and his relationship with these churches (I get into detail in my book, *All That Is Seen And Unseen: A Journey Through The Book Of Revelation*), it is worth pointing out that the book of Revelation and especially the way the Apostle John addresses these churches brings to light an important aspect to the work of the apostle. Apostles and prophets alike have a universal authority, one which is

---

KEY VERSE: REVELATION 3:7

He who has an ear, let him hear what the Spirit says to the churches. To the one who conquers I will grant to eat of the tree of life, which is in the paradise of God. (ESV)

recognizable anywhere they go, anywhere in the world. Even though it may not always be advisable to exercise such authority,

Ephesus

To the angel of the church in Ephesus write: 'The words of Him Who holds the seven stars in His right hand, Who walks among the seven golden lampstands. 'I know your works, your toil and your patient endurance, and how you cannot bear with those who are evil, but have tested those who call themselves apostles and are not, and found them to be false. I know you are enduring patiently and bearing up for My Name's sake, and you have not grown weary. But I have this against you, that you have abandoned the love you had at first. Remember therefore from where you have fallen; repent, and do the works you did at first. If not, I will come to you and remove your lampstand from its place, unless you repent. Yet this you have: you hate the works of the Nicolaitans, which I also hate. He who has an ear, let him hear what the Spirit says to the churches. To the one who conquers I will grant to eat of the tree of life, which is in the paradise of God.' (Revelation 2:1-7, ESV)

The seven letters of Revelation follow a clear mail route, by which mail could be easily distributed and delivered. Ephesus, as the first spot on the trade route, Ephesus was a coastal city. It had a population of about 50,000 people under the Roman Empire, and it was the third largest city in Asia Minor. In addition to its essential status on a trade route, the city was also relevant spiritually, as it was the seat for the pagan Temple of Artemis. This one of the Seven Wonders of the Ancient World was a temple devoted to the Greek goddess Artemis (Diana). We know very little about the devotees of this religion, although from what we do know, it seems to have been a religion devoted to fertility.

The words to Ephesus contain both praise and discipline. Even though the Apostle John was the one who scribed the letter, it was Jesus Who was the true author. This fact is affirmed as Jesus speaks of Himself holding the seven stars (an analogy to the churches and our ability to see dimly this side of heaven. In keeping with this principle, it tells us that what we do, both good and bad, matters to Jesus, and both the good and bad are seen in heaven.

The church at Ephesus had works. They were a group of people who were quick to labor for the Gospel and knew the importance of doing things for other people. They were patient in their endurance, quick to turn away from those who were evil, and to test every spirit that came across in leadership that was false. They were a church that knew what to do, when to do it, and how to do it, without becoming weary.

These are all good, notable, and important attributes. They were a church strong in the area of discernment, and they were strong in their works. It's hard to believe that Jesus had anything to say to them that was contrary, but He did. He goes from praise to telling them that they had abandoned their first love, translated in the English Standard Version as "the love you had at first." This is important to understand just what was spoken to the church at Ephesus, because their love is clearly in connection with "the works you did at first." Even though the church at Ephesus was still doing works and was still doing things of note and that were laudable, they weren't doing them with the right motives. They were good works, but they were empty works, done for sport and for show, just to "do them." This relates to their first love, Christ, because if we don't have a right relationship with Christ, we aren't going to live our faith in the way He asks us to.

Many have asked, why did Ephesus lose its first love? Why did they do things with no meaning, having a wrong relationship with God and with Christ? I believe the very thing that made them strong is what weakened them, and that is their gift of discernment. Even though discernment is not the most desired gift of all, especially these days in church, it is a much needed and very difficult gift to have. It gets tiresome to try so many spirits and find so many people false or lacking the spirituality they claim to have. Seeing so many false spirits mixed in with true ones gets wearying after awhile. Having that gift and seeing so many opportunities to use it became tiresome after awhile and caused the church at Ephesus to lose their faith.

It's easy to point fingers and judge them, but there are many out there, in the world today, who are tired laborers, doing the exterior works with no love or enthusiasm behind them. Doing things just to do them is just as wrong as doing them with the wrong motives. Why we do what we do is just as important as what we are doing. Ephesus should cause us all to stop and look at our own works and our relationship with God. If we aren't doing enough, we need to step it up. If we are doing things but there is no heart behind it, we need to look at why. Ephesus calls us to examine our relationship with works, change what needs changing, and do all we do in His Name, for Him, with Him at the root.

Smyrna

And to the angel of the church in Smyrna write: 'The words of the first and the last, Who died and came to life. 'I know your tribulation and your poverty (but you are rich) and the slander of those who say that they are Jews and are not, but are a synagogue of Satan. Do not fear what you are about to suffer. Behold, the devil is about to throw some of you into prison, that you may be tested, and for ten days you will have tribulation. Be faithful unto death, and I will give you the crown of life. He who has an ear, let him hear what the Spirit says to the churches. The one who conquers will not be hurt by the second death.' (Revelation 2:8-11, ESV)

Smyrna's tone is radically different than that of Ephesus. For one, the church at Smyrna doesn't receive any criticism, only praise and encouragement, for their situation. Smyrna was an ancient costal city, noted for prominence during ancient times. It was considered a prominent city during Roman times and had a strong pagan Greek influence.

Despite all this, the church at Smyrna had other issues. They were a "poor" church, located in a poverty area. They, like most poor churches, had to struggle for what they had. Despite this fact, the church was not spiritually poor, but was spiritually rich! Smyrna had something money couldn't buy, something powerful and important that would carry them from day to day and year to year without having to worry that their souls were in jeopardy of falling from their faith, because their faith was never an issue of question.

Being of faith meant they had a reputation among those who were false. They were attacked by those who claimed to be spiritual, but were not, and they were about to encounter a trial and tribulation. They were encouraged to hold fast, not to lose their faith, to be faithful even unto death, and there they would find the crown of life that would never pass away.

Smyrna reminds us to pay attention to the "ghetto churches," the churches in poorer areas that do not have lots of money and may not have as much of a cosmetic appeal as another church somewhere else. We need to pay attention to inner-city churches that don't have much in the way of money, but are quick to assist the poor and needy, to live their faith, and to move with the Spirit as they are inspired to do so. Even though such may encounter persecution, it is safe to say that God is in places where they recognize all the things money can't buy.

Pergamum

And to the angel of the church in Pergamum write: 'The words of Him Who has the sharp two-edged sword. 'I know where you dwell, where Satan's throne is. Yet you hold fast My Name, and you did not deny My faith even in the days of Antipas My faithful witness, who was killed among you, where Satan dwells. But I have a few things against you: you have some there who hold the teaching of Balaam, who taught Balak to put a stumbling block before the sons of Israel, so that they might eat food sacrificed to idols and practice sexual immorality. So also you have some who hold the teaching of the Nicolaitans. Therefore repent. If not, I will come to you soon and war against them with the sword of My mouth. He who has an ear, let him hear what the Spirit says to the churches. To the one who conquers I will give some of the hidden manna, and I will give him a white stone, with a new name written on the stone that no one knows except the one who receives it. (Revelation 2:12-17, ESV)

Pergamum was a diverse city with many influences, including Egyptian, Persian, Greek, and Roman. There were multiple temples in the city, but the main temple was to Zeus, the most supreme of the Greek gods. This was known as "Satan's throne," as it was a seat of a particular martyrdom, that of Antipas, a bishop appointed by the Apostle John over that city. The church at Pergamum clearly had its work cut out for it. They held fast in this staunchly pagan atmosphere, where they watched a leader fall to the martyrdom of the culture that surrounded the church. Holding fast and not denying the faith must not have been easy, but they did it and persevered in it, nonetheless.

Jesus doesn't leave it there, however. He states that there are some in the church that hold to the teaching of Balaam. Balaam was an Old Testament prophet who was a genuine prophet who was sent to put a "stumbling block" in the way of the Israelites, as inspired by Balak, who was a king. As a result of the stumbling block, the Israelites were led into sin. When someone holds to the teaching of Balaam, they are causing others to sin by their teachings. The words of Revelation don't specify what does say the specific sins in question, and this was on purpose. It doesn't matter what sin someone falls into as the result of such a teaching, the problem is that they were led into sin at all and they now have stumbled before God because of something false that they were taught. The obvious concern for the church at Pergamum was everyone's stumbling, falling into the sin of idolatry and eating food offered to idols (partaking of idolatry in that specific way). They also had some who were a part of the teaching of the Nicolaitans, which was of specific concern. We don't specifically know what this teaching was, even though there are many theories on it. It was believed to be started by a church leader named Nicolas who led people into a place of heresy and gathered followers to himself. What he taught is of debate, but whatever it was, it was serious enough and of enough concern for it to be mentioned as a false teaching no one should follow. It is clear that it was something that came out from among the church, but is not of the church, thus causing it to sound right, look right, be embraced by many as a right teaching or be done by right people, but was not, in reality, real.

Pergamum was staunchly ordered to repent. Despite the things they had and were doing right, they needed to repent and turnaround from the direction they were going that was wrong. If they did not repent, Jesus Himself would come and war against them.

The church at Pergamum reminds us of the importance of holding fast to His Name, and not denying the faith, no matter where we are. It also reminds us that everything we do matters before God. Following false teachers, engaging in false practices, adopting the principles of idols (in any way, shape, or form - not just the big statues people worship in other countries), and causing other people to stumble into sin are all things that are worthy of repentance. Recognizing that everything we do is woven together rather than adopting a spiritually 'separate and secular" identity within ourselves, Pergamum shows that everything we do is interconnected. If we are holding fast to the faith and yet entertaining these other thoughts and actions, we are not going to be able to stand as members of His Body. Holding to one set of rules in one vain and then holding to beliefs that are counter to them tells us clearly that our faith will wind up in trouble if we persist in such double-minded behavior.

> **AUTHOR'S REFLECTIONS**
>
> When reading the book of Revelation, what speaks to you? It's a shame that Revelation is often taught in such a limited, futuristic light. What does God want to say to you in the book of Revelation right now?

These first three churches of Revelation give us a great deal of food for thought in our own personal examinations of ourselves. The issues they faced we face today, even though we might face them in different ways. We still live in a world that often fails to support our beliefs, and we still deal with the choice to leave and follow false teachers or stay and persevere in truth. We have the choice to cause others to stumble or help them stay on the narrow path that leads to life. In our next edition, we will look at the churches of Thyatira, Sardis, Philadelphia, and Laodicea, and hear what God desires to speak to us through them in this season of time.

The Seven Churches of Revelation, Part 2
(Volume 13, Number 4 – Fourth Quarter 2015)

In our last edition of *Power For Today*, we examined the first three of the seven churches of Revelation and also a little bit about why Revelation was written and about the Apostle John's work with the churches. In it, we went over a few basics about the book of Revelation and about the letters to the churches:

1. Revelation was written to the church, not to the world. That means the details of Revelation were written so the church could see itself in prophetic history and recognize different signs and happenings as the church not only perseveres through, but is positioned for victory in history.

2. If Revelation was written to the world, that means that it isn't a book that we use for evangelization. It isn't something that we take to convince the world that it needs to find Jesus. It is something to give us footing and assurance and be aware of our place in prophecy.

3. The seven churches addressed were not addressed by accident.

They are not eras of church history, but they are the church. They represent the problems and issues that the church faces throughout time, even today.

4. Revelation is not all about the future. Even though some of it seems to be written in a futuristic context, it's not all about the future. Revelation is about all of time, the church past, present, and future. Much of Revelation's contents exist right now, in the spiritual realm, even though we can't see it all.

5. God speaks to us through revelation, revealing essential things that we need to know, as a church, because we are important and do matter to God.

> **BEHIND THE ARTICLE**
>
> I had so much material on the seven churches of Revelation that we had to do the cover article in two editions of our magazine. This second one reviews the churches examined in the first edition (Ephesus, Smyrna and Pergamum) and explores the final four (Thyatira, Sardis, Philadelphia and Laodicea).

I believe that one of the greatest undiscovered, yet underlying themes of the book of Revelation is just how important the church is in the sight of God. God cared enough about the church to prove to each and every one of us who are a part of it that it is, indeed, a part of prophecy and a part of His unique plan for mankind. If we grab a hold of this for ourselves, Revelation speaks so much to us on so many different and deep levels.

This month, we are going to look at four of the seven churches of Revelation. Before we get into that, however, here is a recap of the three we discussed in our last edition.

Ephesus, Smyrna and Pergamum

Ephesus, the first church mentioned, received praise and discipline from Jesus. They were a church with great works, who knew how to labor for the Gospel and who recognized that they needed to be of service to other people. They were patient, enduring, quick to turn away from evil people, and they knew how to test spirits. They mastered the fine art of doing all these things and doing them without becoming weary.

Many of us looking at our own churches today might say to ourselves, what could possibly be wrong with a church like this? They sound like everything that too often, our churches are not. Well, no doubt, these are great attributes, and important components of being in church. But this is not all that God had to say to the church at Ephesus. They were told that they abandoned their first love, the "love you had at first," as the English Standard Version puts it. Even though the church at Ephesus did everything right, they weren't doing it with the right heart. They were just doing it to do it, and that was as wrong as not doing it at all.

The church at Ephesus should cause all of us to look at our own relationship with Christ and at the love we have for Him and for others as we do what we are doing. If we are doing it in His Name, then it must be done with His heart, and that is our love, as a part of what we do. In a world that is quick to hope, pray, and push for us to be people that do things, Ephesus reminds us to slow down and make sure we are doing things for the right reasons.

The church at Smyrna doesn't receive any criticism. They only received praise from God, and words of encouragement. Smyrna was a coastal area, and apparently the church there wasn't the richest church in existence. They had financial problems, like many churches do today. They were located in a poverty area, a location that many would compare to the "ghetto" today. They had to struggle for what they had, and they also, most likely, had to struggle to stay open. What God tells Smyrna, however, is not that they lack favor! They are not criticized for being financially poor or compared to other churches. No! They are told that they are spiritually rich! This church had something money couldn't buy. They were not in jeopardy of falling away from their faith, and they were upholding what God required of them. They knew who they were in Christ, and they knew who Christ was, in the midst of them.

The church at Smyrna was being prepared for trial to come, in the very near future. They prove that we can do all the right things and still encounter trials. They were told to hold fast, not lose faith, and remain faithful. The crown of life awaits those who do just that. Smyrna reminds us to pay attention to those churches that don't have much in the material realm but are rich in faith. They have much to offer us, as examples of survivors in faith.

The church at Pergamum was the last church we explored in our look at the seven churches of Revelation in our last edition. We were able to explore how difficult it must have been for the Christians there to remain true to the faith. It was a pagan seat, with a large temple and a lot of pagan

KEY VERSE: REVELATION 3:19-20

Those whom I love, I reprove and discipline, so be zealous and repent. Behold, I stand at the door and knock. If anyone hears my voice and opens the door, I will come in to him and eat with him, and he with Me. (ESV)

activity. The church there was good at holding fast to the Name of Jesus and not forsaking their faith, which was a big accomplishment. That, however, was not all that God had to say to Pergamum. Concerns are raised over those who hold to the teachings of Baalam, which, most likely, were related to causing others to stumble in manner of idolatry. They were also disciplined against adopting the doctrine of the Nicolatians, which we don't even know for sure what it was. It was important enough to be mentioned, which means whatever it was, it mattered to God. Pergamum was staunchly urged to repent, and to change their ways away from what they were doing wrong.

Thyatira

And to the angel of the church in Thyatira write: 'The words of the Son of God, Who has eyes like a flame of fire, and whose feet are like burnished bronze. 'I know your works, your love and faith and service and patient endurance, and that your latter works exceed the first. But I have this against you, that you tolerate that woman Jezebel, who calls herself a prophetess and is teaching and seducing my servants to practice sexual immorality and to eat food sacrificed to idols. I gave her time to repent, but she refuses to repent of her sexual immorality. Behold, I will throw her onto a sickbed, and those who commit adultery with her I will throw into great tribulation, unless they repent of her works, and I will strike her children dead. And all the churches will know that I am He Who searches mind and heart, and I will give to each of you according to your works. But to the rest of you in Thyatira, who do not hold this teaching, who have not learned what some call the deep things of Satan, to you I say, I do not lay on you any other burden. Only hold fast what you have until I come. The one who conquers and who keeps My works until the end, to him I will give authority over the nations, and he will rule them with a rod of iron, as when earthen pots are broken in pieces, even as I myself have received authority from My Father. And I will give him the morning star. He who has an ear, let him hear what the Spirit says to the churches.' (Revelation 2:18-28, ESV)

Next in our churches is the church in Thyatira. In contrast to Smyrna, Thyatira was a wealthy community. It was not a part of a trade route but was known for its extensive artisans' guilds and for dying of fabrics for the rich. The artisan guilds of the city were tightly interwoven with the pagan belief systems, and several paid homages to various deities. In seeing the ancient world and the way that ancients viewed their spiritual lives, there was no division between one's job and one's spirituality. Everything was connected to the various pagan gods, which made the lines of work, what one could do and not do a maze of discernment and confusion for believers who wanted to partake in the luxuries and prosperities of the city itself.

Thyatira is lauded for works, love, faith, service, and patient endurance. Jesus acknowledges that they are doing more now than they did at first and recognizes the importance in the things they are doing right. There is one very, very serious issue among the church at Thyatira, however. This church was tolerating a prophetess, Jezebel, who was misleading the people of God. This is most likely a female oracle that sat in a pagan temple in Thyatira, speaking on behalf of the Sibyl present there. Being this was a pagan woman, she encouraged pagan devotions: eating food sacrificed to idols, sexual fertility rites, and pagan beliefs. Tolerating this woman led to confusion in the church, and a further lack of discernment when it came to spiritual things. The false prophetess was given time to repent, but she refused to do so.

Those who followed her would follow her fate, which was calamity and death. This sounds harsh, but given the face of repentance, and the fact that our long-suffering God probably didn't give just one chance to repent, it's obvious He wanted the people of the church to take things seriously...and get with the problem. He gives to all according to their works, still, forever, eternally. That's why we are to hold to the end, holding to the right works. That proves us righteous to rule, along with Him, as we hold a seat of authority and hear what the Spirit says to the churches.

Sardis

And to the angel of the church in Sardis write: 'The words of Him Who has the seven spirits of God and the seven stars. I know your works. You have the reputation of being alive, but you are dead. Wake up, and strengthen what *remains and is about to die, for I have not found your works complete in the sight of my God. Remember, then, what you received and heard. Keep it, and repent. If you will not wake up, I will come like a thief, and you will not know at what hour I will come against you. Yet you have still a few names in Sardis, people who have not soiled their garments, and they will walk with me in white, for they are worthy. The one who conquers will be clothed thus in white garments, and I will never blot his name out of the book of life. I will confess his name before my Father and before his angels. He who has an ear, let him hear what the Spirit says to the churches.'* (Revelation 3:1-6, ESV)

Sardis was the capital of Lydia, and it was known for its military strength. The facts about what the church in Sardis teach us are basic: reputations are not always true. The church at Sardis had a name which indicated they were alive...yet they were not. Jesus did not address the deception in their name lightly. They were told to strengthen what remains but was about to die. Their works did not stand before the sight of God. They needed to repent, and change their ways, or Jesus Himself would come, taking what needed to be removed, unto the end of the church.

Many teach that Jesus' words were harshest to the church at Laodicea. I do not agree with this. I believe Sardis received Jesus' harshest rebuke, because the very nature of their work was deceptive. They were urged to change before it was too late. Sardis reminds us of the importance of being who we really are - and being true to our nature, not just putting on a good show for those who casually come by.

Philadelphia

And to the angel of the church in Philadelphia write: 'The words of the holy one, the true one, who has the key of David, Who opens and no one will shut, who shuts and no one opens. 'I know your works. Behold, I have set before you an open door, which no one is able to shut. I know that you have but little power, and yet you have kept My Word and have not denied My Name. Behold, I will make those of the synagogue of Satan who say that they are Jews and are not, but lie—behold, I will make them come and bow down before your feet, and they will learn that I have loved you. Because you have kept My Word about patient endurance, I will keep you from the hour of trial that is coming on the whole world, to try those who dwell on the earth. I am coming soon. Hold fast what you have, so that no one may seize your crown. The one who conquers, I will make him a pillar in the temple of My God. Never shall he go out of it, and I will write on him the name of My God, and the name of the city of My God, the new Jerusalem, which comes down from My God out of heaven, and My own new Name. He who has an ear, let him hear what the Spirit says to the churches.' (Revelation 3:7-13, ESV)

The church at Philadelphia is generally known as the church that did right and is typically the one raised up as an example of the "perfect church." They are believed to be a church that only received praise from Jesus. I don't know that I would say the church at Philadelphia was praised as much as encouraged. It's clear that the focus in their letter is different than the others, and rather than being a long list of praises and corrections, the focus is on endurance.

The Bible speaks volumes that they lived their reputation of "brotherly love," particularly in their very Greek, pagan atmosphere. They knew how to keep the Word of God and refrain from denying the Name of Jesus. Those who came among them, who claimed to be one thing but were not, would come back before them and would honor them, seeing that Jesus has loved them. They understood about patient endurance, and for that reason, they would be kept from an hour of trial that was advancing over the earth. The church at Philadelphia was encouraged to hold fast, to conquer, and to be placed as a pillar - as something foundational that holds the temple up, the place of worship, and as having the name of the New Jerusalem upon their foreheads, signifying they belong to it - and there.

Laodicea

And to the angel of the church in Laodicea write: 'The words of the Amen, the faithful and true witness, the beginning of God's creation. 'I know your works: you are neither cold nor hot. Would that you were either cold or hot! So, because you are lukewarm, and neither hot nor cold, I will spit you out of My mouth. For you say, I am rich, I have prospered, and I need nothing, not realizing that you are wretched, pitiable, poor, blind, and naked. I counsel you to buy from me gold refined by fire, so that you may be rich, and white garments so that you may clothe yourself and the shame of your nakedness may not be seen, and salve to anoint your eyes, so that you may see. Those whom I love, I reprove and discipline, so be zealous and repent. Behold, I stand at the door and knock. If anyone hears my voice and opens the door, I will come in to him and eat with him, and he with me. The one who conquers, I will grant him to sit with me on my throne, as I also conquered and sat down with my Father on His throne. He who has an ear, let him hear what the Spirit says to the churches.' (Revelation 3:14-22, ESV)

The last church mentioned among the seven churches is that of Laodicea, probably the church with the worst reputation ever. If you listen to preachers today, many consider the modern church to be of the "era" of Laodicea. Believers of all sorts in our modern times get lumped as "Laodiceans," accused of being lukewarm and not really zealous in their faith. Is this accurate?

Laodicea was a rich, prosperous city. It had Syrian and Jewish influences, rather than Greek. It had a similar layout to Rome, in that it was set on seven hills and it was known as an important center for coin mintage and trade. Yet, Jesus was able to tell all He needed to about the community of believers in this city by their deeds. It wasn't about how great their worship was, or how loud they could sing, or how quickly they started running around the room. Jesus knew that the actions (or lack of) of this church spoke louder than words. He also knew why they felt the way that they did. The church at Laodicea put their confidence in the things of this world: their money, their prosperity, and their exteriors.

Jesus desires us to be a church that is more than just surface deep. I believe that, as with all things pertaining to these churches, no one church is entirely one way or another. All churches have believers in them that could be classified as "lukewarm." There are always people who go to church, meeting the description found above: seeking to look right, to play the part, to declare themselves as faithful so that they can get from God or get acclaim from others. There are always people who claim to believe in Christ but have their true faith in something else. Laodicea shows us how this mindset causes us to have faith in things, rather than in God, and that loving money leads us astray, every single time.

To Laodicea, Jesus urges them to receive from Him, that which is true, and that which will last. The things they had clothed themselves in and trusted in blinded their eyes and pushed them into a place of nakedness, of shame, as is reminiscent of the Garden of Eden. Rather than speaking in anger or hatred, Jesus spoke in correction, reminding us that those He loves, He corrects.

Jesus stands at the door and knocks. Just like He did with Laodicea, He still stands and knocks today, waiting to come in and dine with us. Every person who needs to repent still have the chance to do so. Every person who is lukewarm has the chance to turn and change directions...and to sup with our Savior.

> **AUTHOR'S REFLECTIONS**
>
> When you go to a church, what churches of Revelation do you see present there? More importantly, when you hear the words of Jesus to the churches, what do you hear about yourself?

Words for the Church today

It's easy to read the words of Revelation and try to assign them to a different time, a different era...or maybe more relevantly, someone else's church. We always go through the seven churches of Revelation, looking for them to represent some other time, or some other person, and we often, with haste, think to ourselves, "This sounds like..." What we need to do is some serious - and deep self-examination when it comes to church and where we are as a church, as well as where we are attending church and where we are as individual believers. The seven churches of Revelation remind us that God is a part of our lives, whether we acknowledge Him present therein in the way we need to, or not. God is watching...are you called to repent...endure...praise...or something else? If you have ears...hear!

21 UNITY
(Volume 9, Number 6—June 2010)

I recently started reading the book, *Raising the Ruins: The Fight to Revive the Legacy of Herbert W. Armstrong* by Stephen Flurry. While not an advocate of the doctrines pertaining to Armstrongism, I have always been very intrigued by this group. Even within a state of intrigue, I could never figure out what it was about them that intrigued me until I started reading this book. It's not their doctrine, their structure, or even their lifestyles. What so intrigues me about the Armstrong Movement is its total lack of unity. Here is a movement, founded on a strong, charismatic leader. For the most part, the leadership never questioned the doctrine until after Herbert Armstrong's death. Once Herbert Armstrong died - and somewhat for years before - the top leaders of his denomination all vied for control of the church. Everyone thought they were the best choice to replace their original leader. In reading the discourses, situations, and different dialogues, it sounds like a bunch of children fighting over who got to be club leader. It did not help matters when the individual selected to replace Herbert W. Armstrong moved in and moved out those who believed they should have been selected as leader. The church politics disrupted into chaos, with several fraction churches breaking from the original church, seeking to establish their own leadership separate from the changes made to Armstrong's original movement.

I can understand where members of the church would feel betrayed by the doctrinal changes forced upon them under the new administration following Herbert Armstrong's death. Whether right or wrong, a whole church of people believed in certain doctrines that they upheld, and all accepted with a certain degree of personal certainty. To have a new administration swoop in and change everything around without study, consultation, or evaluation from anyone is certainly wrong. Yet, at the same time, isn't it just as wrong for the debating leaders to fight over who will be in charge?

> **BEHIND THE ARTICLE**
>
> The book I was reading at the time I wrote this article inspired not just this writing, but also an audio teaching that can be downloaded as an .mp3 file online.

The fact that only one human being was ever able to successfully lead the Worldwide Church of God speaks volumes to the establishment of the church and its true foundations. It also speaks loudly that individuals were united under a central human leader instead of Jesus Christ. In modern times, "unity" has become the Christian buzzword designed to cause extremes: everything from abandoning doctrinal truth to justifying controlling leadership. In the midst of ecumenical tolerance and thousands of different denominational divisions, what is the truth about church unity? How does the true church show its unity? Most importantly, how can God's church become unified?

What is unity?

The word "unity" has been tossed around casually by individuals of differing belief systems for about fifty years. While different Christian denominations engaged in dialogue and discussion for nearly one hundred years prior to the development of modern unity movements, Christian unity was an avoided topic. The different denominations and divisions within Christianity meant so much to their leaders and followers that members of denominations stood behind doctrinal differences. While no one doubted they had things in common with other Christian denominations, no one denied their differences, either. Unity was something Christians did not seek; they simply believed they were unified within their denominations and left matters at that.

The belief that unity was necessary changed with the rise of the Ecumenical and Interfaith Movements. These movements pushed for dialogue and unity rooted in commonalities among cross-denominations and even among those of different faith traditions. The focus of such dialogues was to put aside differences of doctrine - viewing the differences as opinions - and focus instead on the commonalities - which were regarded as truth. Years and years of such attitudes about essential matters of faith have caused people to believe unity is a matter of doctrinal compromise and ignoring differences. If we understand the Word, this extreme certainly cannot be the definition of unity!

In the midst of such disorder, many denominations and smaller ministries rose up, proclaiming themselves to have truth in only one place - their church or ministry. Leaders strong in nature, dominant in attitude, and with a thorough heart to control, proclaim themselves the only and exclusive way to reach God. If you don't attend their church, ministry, or follow them, you are not in unity with truth. To these leaders, unity is only achievable through their human leadership. As we saw in the example of Herbert Armstrong above, unity was certainly not an achievement of his church! The same can be said of any powerful, charismatic leader. While people may come together because they agree with something someone says or does, living under a controlled leadership setting is not the answer to unity.

These extremes represent two chief attitudes about unity today. Many people also believe unity is an impossibility due to our many differences, or that unity is achievable, but they are unsure how it is possible. With so many concepts, just what is unity?

Unity is something we grow into as we begin to understand it in a deeper sense. As we grow spiritually, we grow into a greater unity with God and, ideally, with others who are also growing spiritually and gaining greater unity with their Heavenly Father. Yet we can't walk in unity if we don't understand it, and we can't apply it if we don't know how it relates to us as believers.

In John 17:20-26, Jesus prays the following prayer: *My prayer is not for them alone. I pray also for those who will believe in Me through their message, that all of them may be one, Father, just as you are in Me and I am in You. May they also be in us so that the world may believe that you have sent Me. I have given them the glory that you gave Me, that they may be one as We are one: I in them and you in Me. May they be brought to complete unity to let the world know that You sent Me and have loved them even as you have loved Me. Father, I want those you have given Me to be with me where I am, and to see My glory, the glory you have given Me because You loved me before the creation of the world. Righteous Father, though the world does not know You, I know You, and they know that You have sent Me. I have made You known to them, and will continue to make*

KEY VERSE: EPHESIANS 4:3

Make every effort to keep the unity of the Spirit through the bond of peace.

You known in order that the love You have for Me may be in them and that I Myself may be in them. Even though this passage is seldom studied, Jesus reveals to us a great many things about what unity is and how it applies to us as believers.

First, we can make one important conclusion: if Jesus prayed for us to be unified as believers, it is a possibility. Unity is neither impossible, nor is it unattainable due to differences. Jesus fully well knew the Christian church would include many diverse cultures, backgrounds, histories, languages, and nations; yet He still put forth the importance for us to be unified. How is this achieved?

Second, we learn how unity is achieved: we must be one in Christ. This means we put aside the flesh and grow up in Spirit to become Christ-like in our character and nature. We must not seek to make the Body of Christ a selfish, self-centered organization that is all about us; but we must be one in Christ and with Christ. We put ourselves aside to achieve Christ's purpose.

Third, we must unite in a common goal. Unity for the sake of nothing is ineffective. We can't say we'll all unite and then stand for nothing. As a rule, unity makes people uncomfortable for this reason: unity mandates us to make a choice about what we believe and whether or not we are willing to stand for it. In Christ, our common purpose is the Gospel. We are about proclaiming the good news to the world and letting all know how they may be set free. In Him, our common interest is advancing the Kingdom of God through our Gospel living and proclamation. Through unity, we also recognize we share a common experience. Even though we are not all the same, we do not have the same culture, speak the same language, or live through the same challenges, we all live in Christ and from that focal point, we all have experiences that are sometimes similar to one another.

Fourth, we recognize unity is only achieved through love. Not only must we recognize God's love manifest through Christ, but we must also accept it and walk in it. As we do so, we grow in the love of Christ one to another. This love is the source of our interest, concern, and lack of jealousy or envy among true believers who are past the point of walking in the flesh.

Lastly, we see in this passage how important unity is in our proclamation of the Gospel to the world. A disunified, argumentative, fleshly church does not have the necessary impact to turn hearts toward the Father in repentance. A church united in Christ is a true witness that Jesus is real, the love of God is true, and salvation is obtainable as the gift of God through Jesus Christ.

What is unity? It is the church working as the Body of Christ with Christ as our Head. It is many diverse people coming together and working together not for personal goals, but for the Gospel.

Now that we know what unity is, how do we know who to unite to?

Doctrines that unify

Most denominations adhere to a standard book of doctrinal essentials. In order to be a member of their church, you must ascribe to their "essentials" of faith. When it comes to unity, however, the Bible has already established for us the "essentials of faith" on which we build unity in the Body of Christ. These teachings are found in Ephesians 4:1-6: *As a prisoner for the Lord, then, I urge you to live a life worthy of the calling you have received. Be completely humble and gentle; be patient, bearing with one another in love. Make every effort to keep the unity of the Spirit through the bond of peace. There is one body and one Spirit—just as you were called to one hope when you were called— one Lord, one faith, one baptism; one God and Father of all, who is over all and through all and in all.* While the Apostle Paul made this passage very understandable and simple in its wording, he has also laid out for us the very foundation of our faith. Within that foundation are the conditions of doctrinal unity. As the heart of God is to unite believers, we learn about the essentials of faith: Live a life worthy of the calling we received (that call unto salvation and eternal life), be humble, gentle, and patient (allow God to teach and work in us, walking and modeling those qualities as we deal with others), bearing with one another in love. As we exemplify these qualities, we see they are truly the basis for us learning the truth and uniting with other believers in the truth. We are commanded to keep the unity of the Spirit through the bond of peace. This tells us we must believe in the Spirit, the Holy Spirit, as more than an ancient musing active in Bible times. If the Holy Spirit is the source of our unity, we find the gifts of the Spirit to be an essential and integral part of unifying the body. As we all work together, walking in the gifts given to us by God, we all come to a greater sense of unity because we are walking not just for ourselves, but the advance of the Kingdom.

The more specific points of doctrine are mentioned next: we recognize one body and one Spirit, which clearly establishes one thing: the Body of Christ is not about denominations or beliefs built by men. There is but one church in Christ and we are His members because we recognize only one uniting Spirit, the Holy Spirit. The one hope we all recognize is salvation, to which we were called. In Christ, we recognize Him as our only Lord, and none other; we recognize one faith that saves, which is in Him; we recognize one baptism, symbolic of our death to sin and rising to new life in Christ; and one God and Father of us all. We do not accept a plurality of gods or worship of a false god, and we recognize that God is omnipresent, working in and through circumstances, and working in and through those of us about His Kingdom business.

Unifying leadership

> **AUTHOR'S REFLECTIONS**
>
> When the topic of unity comes up in a church setting, it becomes one of my least favorite topics to discuss with others. Why? Because we don't properly take the time to step back and understand what it is and how it should manifest in our lives and in our congregations. If your first question about unity is who is in charge, then that tells me you have not become spiritual enough to understand true unity in your own walk.

Ephesians 4 goes on to provide to us the leadership structure established by God designed for unity: *But to each one of us grace has been given as Christ apportioned it. This is why it says: 'When He ascended on high, He led captives in His train and gave gifts to men.' (What does "he ascended" mean except that he also descended to the lower, earthly regions? He Who descended is the very One Who ascended higher than all the heavens, in order to fill the whole universe.) It was He Who gave some to be apostles, some to be prophets, some to be evangelists, and some to be pastors and teachers, to prepare God's people for works of service, so that the body of Christ may be built up until we all reach unity in the faith and in the knowledge of the Son of God and become mature, attaining to the whole measure of the fullness of Christ. Then we will no longer be infants, tossed back and forth by the waves, and blown here and there by every wind of teaching and by the cunning and craftiness of men in their deceitful scheming. Instead, speaking the truth in love, we will in all things grow up into Him Who is the Head, that is, Christ. From Him the whole body, joined and held together by every supporting ligament, grows and builds itself up in love, as each part does its work.* (Ephesians 5:7-16) When we follow the leadership pattern God has established, it unifies and strengthens the body, protecting it from evil destructions that seek to destroy it. Every component of leadership mentioned in this passage: equipping, building up, teaching, speaking the truth in love, growing up, and supporting are a part of serving as a unified body. If we ignore God's established leadership, we cannot expect unity to be the result!

Living in unity

Ephesians 4 ends with clear advice designed to maintain the unity of the Body of Christ and stand as a witness to it in everyday life: *So I tell you this, and insist on it in the Lord, that you must no longer live as the Gentiles do, in the futility of their thinking. They are darkened in their understanding and separated from the life of God because of the ignorance* that is in them due to the hardening of their hearts. Having lost all sensitivity, they have given themselves over to sensuality so as to indulge in every kind of impurity, with a continual lust for more. You, however, did not come to know Christ that way. Surely you heard of Him and were taught in Him in accordance with the truth that is in Jesus. You were taught, with regard to your former way of life, to put off your old self, which is being corrupted by its deceitful desires; to be made new in the attitude of your minds; and to put on the new self, created to be like God in true righteousness and holiness. Therefore each of you must put off falsehood and speak truthfully to his neighbor, for we are all members of one body. 'In your anger do not sin': Do not let the sun go down while you are still angry, and do not give the devil a foothold. He who has been stealing must steal no longer, but must work, doing something useful with his own hands, that he may have something to share with those in need. Do not let any unwholesome talk come out of your mouths, but only what is helpful for building others up according to their needs, that it may benefit those who listen. And do not grieve the Holy Spirit of God, with whom you were sealed for the day of redemption. Get rid of all bitterness, rage and anger, brawling and slander, along with every form of malice. Be kind and compassionate to one another, forgiving each other, just as in Christ God forgave you. (Ephesians 4:17-32) Here we find conduct essential for maintaining unity in our daily lives. No more do we act, think, or behave like those who do not know Christ, but we display Christ-like character in everything we do. We treat others as we desire to be treated. We display an attitude of forgiveness. Most of all, in our daily living, we display the new being we have become in Christ.

Ephesians 4 reveals God's perfect plan for church unity. Have you caught the vision yet? If not, don't delay! Unity in Christ is a part of God's plan for your life!

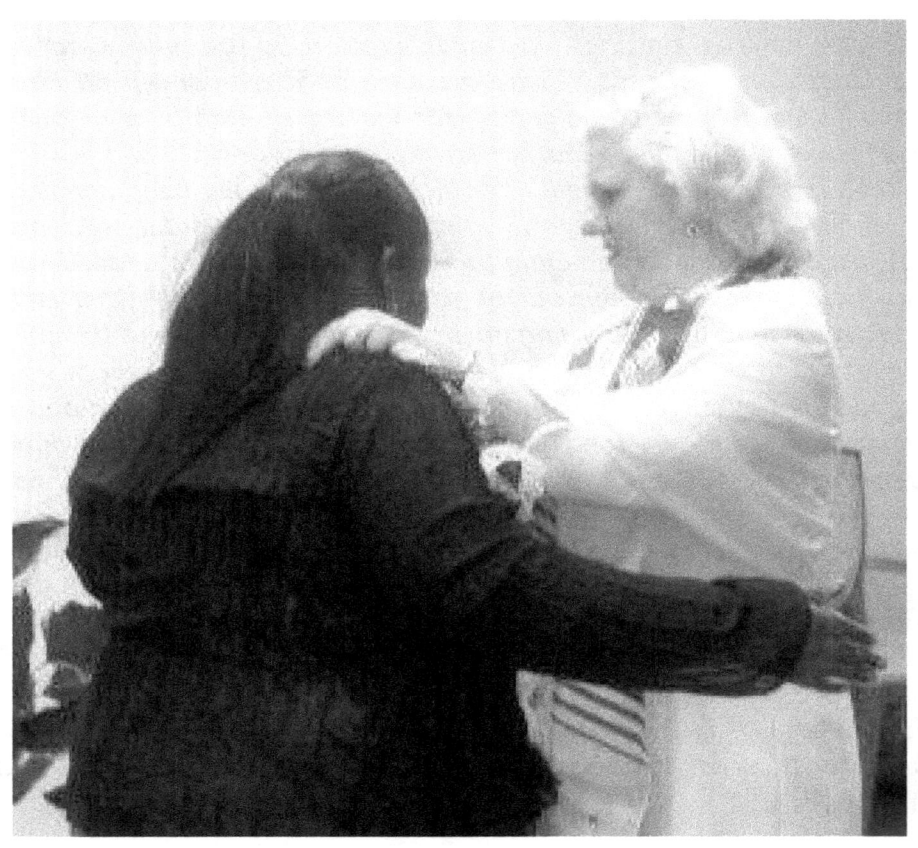

Apostle Marino ministering to a woman at a church in Toms River, New Jersey following an ordination the day before (May 2012)

22 PRAISE GOD ANYWAY!
(Volume 8, Number 4 – April 2009)

Most Christians today report a general dissatisfaction with their faith. They are all waiting for their spiritual breakthrough or for God to bring something to come to pass at all times. As the years go by and the tally of wants to outweigh the tally of answered requests, the majority of Christians begin to grow somewhat embittered against God when they do not receive what they want. Many people enter the Christian faith thinking it is a pass to receive whatever they want, whenever they want, and however they want, and find themselves very disappointed when what they want is not handed over to them. We find a deeply embedded issue recurring of ingratitude as the surest sign that Christians today do not have the first clue about the importance of being thankful and praise filled.

We don't hear a lot of teaching about the power of praise today in churches. There are probably some out there who believe "praise" is a type of music limited to a few songs each service. Most of church teaching focuses on the belief that having what one wants is the inherent right of a Christian. Is this really Biblical teaching? If we truly seek the Scriptures, we can see that endless want is not a characteristic of Christians. This can only mean one of two things: either Christians get everything they want, or they learn how to live content. As we come to study the topic of praise further, we will clearly see it is learning how to live content that is the call of every Christian.

Another popular concept that is heralded in Christian circles is that which looks totally to a better day in which the whole world will praise God because all will be at peace. While we know that Jesus shall return and things as we know them will change, we also must recognize what God is doing RIGHT NOW that is praiseworthy and important. Just because the world isn't perfect doesn't mean that God isn't working.

It's obvious from the attitudes, thoughts, and general dissatisfaction of Christians that praise isn't on their life-map. This means that perhaps millions of people are missing out on a powerful way to handle trials and difficulties. How can we get in on handling such situations? Instead of pouting, whining, and complaining to God all the time about what He's not doing, we are going to praise God anyway despite what we are going through.

> **BEHIND THE ARTICLE**
>
> The topic of "praising God ANYWAY!" became so immensely popular, it turned into a preached message as well as this article. The message form of this teaching is available now as an .mp3 teaching online.

The reality of our worldly situation

1 Thessalonians 5:12-18 tells us: *Now we ask you, brothers, to respect those who work hard among you, who are over you in the Lord and who admonish you. Hold them in the highest regard in love because of their work. Live in peace with each other. And we urge you, brothers, warn those who are idle, encourage the timid, help the weak, be patient with everyone. Make sure that nobody pays back wrong for wrong, but always try to be kind to each other and to everyone else. Be joyful always; pray continually; give thanks in all circumstances, for this is God's will for you in Christ Jesus.* We are given some very noteworthy advice in this passage that is worth examining. Those of us who are Christians are to be a people observant enough to step outside of ourselves and pay attention to the bigger picture that God is orchestrating within the Kingdom. We are to be a people who recognize the accomplishments and work of others and to stand up with warnings when people aren't following God, encouragement when someone is fearful, help for the weak, and a consistent position of not acting in a deceitful or evil manner, even when we are handled with an evil manner. Such consistent behavior calls for us to have consistency in our walk with God. How can we maintain ourselves? Through praise! Verses 16-18 tell us how this is accomplished: We face every situation with

consistent joy, constantly communicate with God, and give thanks in all circumstances because this is God's will for us in Jesus...wait a minute! It says that it is God's will for us to give thanks in ALL circumstances. That's quite a statement if we don't understand it. The Word does not say to give thanks FOR all things, but to give thanks IN all things. This means that despite what we are going through, we can praise God anyway! We cannot let our circumstances dictate our relationship with God because to do so will severely limit the spiritual power that is available to us.

The reality of our times is that the world is not going to get better. We are not going to be able to escape the difficulties of this life. Spiritual maturity is what gets us through those difficult times, as we grow through what we go through. Just like they were called to in the first century New Testament times, so we too are called to reach spiritual maturity, as we grow and change from glory to glory and faith to faith.

Recognizing difficult circumstances

Everyone goes through difficult times. When we look at the Bible with the intent to hear God speaking to us, we can discover that people in the Bible weren't that different from us in this regard. They dealt with life and death, loss and grief, marital problems, family problems, sibling rivalries, difficulties in the world, and fighting off or avoiding enemies. There were two types of people in the Bible: those who continued to trust God and remain faithful to Him despite circumstances and those who did not. We, as believers, are called to draw on the experiences of those in Scripture and look at the results of how each situation was handled. While not everything may have turned out the way someone might have wanted it to turn out, when they stayed faithful in God, things turned out the best for everyone.

One such example is found 2 Corinthians 12:1-10: *I must go on boasting. Although there is nothing to be gained, I will go on to visions and revelations from the Lord. I know a man in Christ who fourteen years ago was caught up to the third heaven. Whether it was in the body or out of the body I do not know—God knows. And I know that this man—whether in the body or apart from the body I do not know, but God knows— was caught up to paradise. He heard inexpressible things, things that man is not permitted to tell. I will boast about a man like that, but I will not boast about myself, except about my weaknesses. Even if I should choose to boast, I*

KEY VERSE: 1 THESSALONIANS 5:1

Give thanks in all circumstances, for this is God's will for you in Christ Jesus.

would not be a fool, because I would be speaking the truth. But I refrain, so no one will think more of me than is warranted by what I do or say. To keep me from becoming conceited because of these surpassingly great revelations, there was given me a thorn in my flesh, a messenger of Satan, to torment me. Three times I pleaded with the Lord to take it away from me. But he said to me, 'My grace is sufficient for you, for My power is made perfect in weakness.' Therefore I will boast all the more gladly about my weaknesses, so that Christ's power may rest on me. That is why, for Christ's sake, I delight in weaknesses, in insults, in hardships, in persecutions, in difficulties. For when I am weak, then I am strong.

In this passage, the Apostle Paul clearly acknowledges a problem he'd had for a number of years. Here he was, an apostle, who had a great revelation experience and yet continued to have a pesky problem. It doesn't say what it was because Paul's thorn in the flesh represents all those pesky problems we all have that don't magically go away because we are Christians with great spiritual experiences. Paul worked through his ministry with other great hardships and difficulties, and in addition to those, he had to live with his "thorn in the flesh;" but that didn't mean he had to surrender to his problem! Notice we never, ever see Paul complaining about his problems to the churches. What he consistently did instead was draw on them and praise God through them.

We can also see that Paul's boast was always in Christ rather than himself. Despite any troubles he might have had, Paul always enjoyed God's favor and revelation for his life. Even though we may not all receive the same type of vision or experience Paul had, we can always realize that God is there for us in so many ways and derive wisdom from our life experiences. Paul's thorn was acknowledged to make him stronger and see God's power work more effectively because in those circumstances it forces Paul to grow, mature, and trust God more. Power truly does come as we are perfected through our weaknesses!

The reason for difficult circumstances

Often people lose their power of praise when they spend time trying to analyze a situation. We know from the Word that in and of itself, there is nothing wrong with analyzing a situation that presents itself. When we identify difficult circumstances, it is often the first step to see what we can do to cooperate with God in its ending. We can see, however, in Romans 8:18-25, the overall reason why difficulties exist in this life: *I consider that our present sufferings are not worth comparing with the glory that will be revealed in us. The creation waits in eager expectation for the sons of God to be revealed. For the creation was subjected to frustration, not by its own choice, but by the will of the one who subjected it, in hope that the creation itself will be liberated from its bondage to decay and brought into the glorious freedom of the children of God. We know that the whole creation has been groaning as in the pains of childbirth right up to the present time. Not only so, but we ourselves, who have the firstfruits of the Spirit, groan inwardly as we wait eagerly for our adoption as sons, the redemption of our bodies. For in this hope we were saved. But hope that is seen is no hope at all. Who hopes for what he already has? But if we hope for what we do not yet have, we wait for it patiently.* The reason why we go through difficulties in this world is because there are difficulties here. The whole of creation deals with the difficulties that entered the picture when sin entered the world, and all of creation awaits the day when the present problems will cease. But what gets us through those problems is sticking with God as we come to realize we must praise God anyway because we have the promise of hope that the world doesn't have! No matter how bad things may become, we have that eternal promise of hope as we have read the end of the book; we know what awaits us, and we have to keep on praising God for the hope of that eternal promise!

The power in praise

Throughout God's Word we can clearly see the greatest power we find in praise is that God is our praise. A believer's focus should always reflect that God is the reason we have anything at all! As interesting as science may be, it's not thanks to science that we have the earth we live in, it's thanks to God. As interesting as medicine may be, it's not thanks to medicine that we have miracles, it's thanks to God. It's mindful for us to always keep this focus when going through the different situations life brings. We can all remember how well we did on our own when we tried to run our lives without God's guidance. Most of us lived in total messes, and our problems mounted as we created new problems in the hopes we could resolve the old problems. Because of this realization, we always have God to praise. He is the reason that we are where we are and even though it may not be where we will wind up, at least it is not the mess we came from. Deuteronomy 10:12-22 provides to us plenty of reasons why it is desirable, lovely, and powerful to praise God: *And now, O Israel, what does the LORD your God ask of you but to fear the LORD your God, to walk in all His ways, to love Him, to serve the LORD your God with all your heart and with all your soul, and to observe the LORD's commands and decrees that I am giving you today for your own good? To the LORD your God belong the heavens, even the highest heavens, the earth and everything in it. Yet the LORD set His affection on your forefathers and loved them, and He chose you, their descendants, above all the nations, as it is today. Circumcise your hearts, therefore, and do not be stiff-necked any longer.*

For the LORD your God is God of gods and Lord of lords, the great God, mighty and awesome, Who shows no partiality and accepts no bribes. He defends the cause of the fatherless and the widow, and loves the alien, giving him food and clothing. And you are to love those who are aliens, for you yourselves were aliens in Egypt. Fear the LORD your God and serve Him. Hold fast to Him and take your oaths in His Name. He is your praise; He is your God, Who performed for you those great and awesome wonders you saw with your own eyes. Your forefathers who went down into Egypt were seventy in all, and now the LORD your God has made you as numerous as the stars in the sky.

> **AUTHOR'S REFLECTIONS**
>
> Praising God no matter what is going on in our lives is not something that we always feel like doing. If we are going to be serious believers, however, it is something absolutely necessary to take us into our spiritual development and gain important perspective into what God wants to do in and through us.

Look at all we can rightly praise God for! We can praise God because of creation, the earth that we have and all the resources in it. We can praise God because while we may measure ourselves next to others, the world may judge us unworthy, but God has called and chosen us anyway! We learn that God defends and cares for those who are viewed as helpless or hopeless; in His infinite mercy, God gives them hope! He performs great and mighty wonders that nobody can understand! It is God that multiplies us - not in a reproductive sense now but by adding to our Kingdom numbers! Praise God for His marvels!

We can see here that there is a great power in praise because praise not only connects us to God, it also calls to mind recall of all God has done and is doing. Praise reminds us of our place in God's presence and all we can and rightly should do because God has been so good to us. It is for this reason that we see the reminder to be good to aliens and strangers among us; more than anything, God is reminding us of the importance to be consistent across the board, treating believer and non-believer alike with respect and dignity because it brings praise and glory unto Him.

Praise as a spiritual defense against the enemy

When we stop praising God, we give the enemy full access to our lives because we start opening doors for him. Praise is an expression of our faith; and if we stop expressing our faith through praise, the temptation exists to abandon faith all together. There is a lot of truth to the fact that if we don't praise God in the wilderness, we won't praise Him when we get to the Promised Land. For this reason, it is essential that we make the point, no matter how difficult things may be, to praise God in all He is because all He is, is enough to praise!

Praise also serves as a spiritual defense against depression, lack of spiritual zeal, loss of faith, and failure to have a life-changing testimony. Nobody likes to be around a moaner, including those who are doing the moaning. If we want to be strong in our faith and avoid spiritual pitfalls as we go along, we must remain strong in our praise.

Pray in the Spirit

Ephesians 6:18 gives us a key to praise: *Pray in the Spirit for all things.* This includes the prayer of praise not just for what God is doing for us individually, but what God is doing for us all. Prayer and praising are a part of spiritual warfare because every praise given to God is a victory over the enemy, reminding the enemy that his days are numbered. We also see from praise that our troubles are numbered! Don't make the mistake of thinking praise makes no difference. Praise brings change in focus, heart, spirit, and mind. This is why it is such a cornerstone of the faithful: praise is powerful!

So what do we do? Are you in doubt about something? Praise God and ask for discernment! Are you waiting for God to do something? Praise Him and trust Him for it! Are you in need of His miraculous touch? Praise Him and believe Him for His will in your situation! For every need you have, praise Him! For every situation that brings you closer to Him, praise Him! In praise, remember His faithfulness, and renew your faith and trust knowing He will be faithful to see you through as well. And as we await the time when all shall be restored, hallow the words of Psalm 150:6: *Let everything that has breath praise the LORD. Praise the LORD.*

Apostle Marino preaching in Garner, North Carolina (March 2010)

23 HOSPITALITY
(Volume 10, Number 7–July 2011)

A recent discussion online encouraging ministers to go overseas has caused me to start thinking about the issue of international travel in ministry. The discussion got very interesting as more and more individuals from overseas started making bold requests for people to come over to their groups and assemblies. A discussion that was established to encourage people to start to seek God about going beyond their comfort zones and do His work quickly turned into a commercial for every foreign ministry to, yet again, put out their petition for people to go to their country and do for them. The requests were, and are, always the same: we're doing this and this, you are most welcome to come to our country. There is usually something that comes up about orphans and widows, housing and, of course, the call for money. If we are to go to these countries, the expense, we are told will be ours: we have to pay for our tickets, our hotel and transportation, forward money to cover the events, there will be no offering taken, we will not be compensated in any way for the event, and we are expected to give additional money, as well, to whatever it is they are doing. They ask for everything, from the cost of building a new church to providing books and materials for them at no charge. When the issue of money comes up, they never have any, it's not an option for them to give or cover any costs. The ironic part: they also want to come to the United States...and once again, it's on our dime. Whether we're going or they're coming, the expectation is the same: we pay for them and for what they want to do, and they do not think they should assume any cost. There is expectation without willingness to participate.

When I first started covering people back in 2004, everyone I initially covered was from overseas, specifically, Pakistan, Africa, and India. They all wanted a few things from me: a lot of time, me to send them a lot of materials for free, and to send certificates. A few were as bold as to proclaim themselves my "representatives" in their respective countries. So I provided what I could. Before I knew it, they were gone. We reached a point where they wanted something they didn't get, and then they were gone. Even though I handle things differently now than I used to, the pattern is the same: I am contacted, if I don't meet what someone from certain foreign countries wants, I don't hear from them again.

> **BEHIND THE ARTICLE**
>
> Most people don't post their "least read ever" articles in an anthology, but that is exactly what this article turned out to be. On a highly unpopular topic, it is, to date, my least read edition of *Power For Today* Magazine. Read or not, its value merits its inclusion in our anthology.

I don't want to give the impression that I think every overseas ministry is like this. I know and work with many ministries in various parts of the world and love the people who oversee them dearly. The first person I ever covered is still with me today, seven years later. He is a missionary overseas and has never been a problem. He has even expressed his desire to come and work for our ministry over here. He has not, however, ever expected me to cover that cost. He has expressed that God will provide in His timing. He knows my heart, and I know his, and we both know that when God is ready, He will make the way without the situation presenting a burden. There are many others I adore who I know are doing the work of God, making a difference, and standing for truth. We support one another in prayer, in truth, and in the day when we can work together in person for the work of the Kingdom.

We've seen the pictures on television and are often intrigued to learn of foreign political corruption. As all we ever hear from these countries is the constant cry of "We're poor, support us!" we have grown to assume this is just how it is. If we are called to go, we need to learn more about the who, what, where, when, and why of where we are going, who we are going to, and why we are going there. We need to have a plan. More importantly, we need to know what God is asking of us in these situations. We need to recognize what God asks of ministers, as well as what God asks of those who invite us to minister. We need to see God's command for us to work together and see the partnership in the two.

We need to hear God's call. The church needs to have more of a global outlook. We have become so obsessed with local churches and being a part of a local church that we have lost sight of the rest of the church beyond our own four walls. It becomes a conflict when multiple events happen on a weekend, and we're afraid to consider anything that happens or participate in things for fear that our leaders will grow threatened and angry. We have shrunk ourselves to literal non-existence and impact. At the same time, we need to be careful in what we pursue. God does not ask us to just give anywhere; He asks us to sow. Sow, indeed, in good soil. And the way we determine good soil is by assessing various fruits. The one major fruit we need to examine here is the fruit of hospitality.

I talk about leaders all the time. When we are invited to minister, we need to have a good attitude, not behave unseemly, and not make excessive demands. This doesn't mean we get walked all over or avoid discussions about arrangements and money. I know most of the ministers who will read this have considered preaching overseas and have most likely allowed certain things to stop them. In this article, it's time for us to consider the call of those who invite us: and that call is HOSPITALITY.

What is hospitality?

The word "hospitality" is defined in Strong's Exhaustive Concordance as "Love to strangers; hospitality." It is found in the Bible and is listed as a spiritual gift. In ancient cultures, the level of one's hospitality was considered a serious indicator of the type of person one was. As we can see with Lot and the angels (Genesis 19:1-9), it would have been considered unseemly for him to leave the men on the side of the road or allow harm to come to them. Guests were guarded with one's very life, health, and safety, and all in the name of hospitality.

Hospitality was a way of life, a way people approached their own image and their own assistance to others. It didn't matter how poor they might have been, how difficult things might be for them, or how uncomfortable the situation might become to them: they were going to be hospitable. The story of the poor widow and Elijah (1 Kings 17:8-26) proves this point: she

---

KEY VERSE: LUKE 10:7

And stay on in the same house, eating and drinking what they provide, for the laborer is worthy of his wages. (AMPC)

was afraid her hospitality might cost her more than she could afford, but in her stead, God blessed her hospitality by seeing to it that her needs were met. When we are hospitable, our needs are met, no matter how abundant they may seem to be. No one is exempt, in the name of being poor, from being hospitable.

In the New Testament, we see several examples of hospitality among the first century church: Lydia (Acts 16:14-15) extended herself as a hostess to the Apostle Paul and his companions. The Apostle Paul travelled between churches and took care of himself as those who supported his ministry assisted him (Philippians 4:10-19). The concept of pastoring in one's house is another extension of hospitality (Colossians 4:15). Then there is the major area of hospitality we try to skip today: that of hosting visiting ministers and ministries. Hospitality means that the inviting agency is willing to provide transportation, hotel accommodation, and offering, if not more. In other words: when we invite someone to minister for us, we are willing to do what they can to see their needs are met and are willing to make them as comfortable as possible.

Foreign ministries who expect to receive without any thought to those they invite are not exercising hospitality. They are not extending such because they think being poor exempts them from having to be hospitable - which the Bible does not support. Any ministry that expects to receive with no thought to the expense of the minister is not exercising hospitality, no matter where they may be in the world. If you invite someone to minister for you, you are expected to be hospitable to those who labor among you. How does such hospitality manifest?

Manifesting hospitality

When Jesus commanded first the twelve, and then the seventy, to go out and proclaim the Gospel, He gave them the following instructions: *NOW AFTER this the Lord chose and appointed seventy others and sent them out ahead of Him, two by two, into every town and place where He Himself was about to come (visit). And He said to them, The harvest indeed is abundant [there is much ripe grain], but the farmhands are few. Pray therefore the Lord of the harvest to send out laborers into His harvest. Go your way; behold, I send you out like lambs into the midst of wolves. Carry no purse, no provisions bag, no [change of] sandals; refrain from [retarding your journey by] saluting and wishing anyone well along the way. Whatever house you enter, first say, Peace be to this household! Freedom from all the distresses that result from sin be with this family]. And if anyone [worthy] of peace and blessedness is there, the peace and blessedness you wish shall come upon him; but if not, it shall come back to you. And stay on in the same house, eating and drinking what they provide, for the laborer is worthy of his wages. Do not keep moving from house to house. Whenever you go into a town and they receive and accept and welcome you, eat what is set before you; And heal the sick in it and say to them, The kingdom of God has come close to you.* (Luke 10:1-9, AMPC) The Bible is clear that those who proclaim the Gospel are worthy of receiving hospitality. There is no shame in receiving it, nor does it make a minister all about money. Those who proclaim the Gospel are able to freely proclaim it because they have freely received from those who have heard it. While today we make that verse all about the minister freely proclaiming that message because they have freely received it from God, that verse is more about the hospitality the ministers of God receive, that they may continue to freely give the message. If the ministers in question aren't receiving hospitality, they cannot freely give the message.

In modern society, the way hospitality is extended is a little different than it was in ancient times. The command to be hospitable, however much society has changed, remains the same. Even though the way we are hospitable is different, we are still commanded to do it.

Calling

Contrary to what our inboxes may display, there ARE places in the world that have need of the Gospel besides Africa, India, and Pakistan. There are nations of the world, such as China and Iran, where Christians have no outlet to share their needs due to internet restrictions and various regulations. I don't seek to minimize the suffering of people in nations such as Africa, India, and Pakistan, but we also can't ignore that the rest of the world has needs and there are plenty of us to go everywhere. Not every minister with a call to go and work internationally will be sent to Africa, India, and Pakistan. Some will be sent to nations that are more developed but have deep spiritual needs. Some will be sent to underdeveloped nations with many types of needs. Some go to disaster areas, and some go to places where needs are more spiritual than material. There is no shame in saying, "I appreciate your message, but I am not sent to go to your country." We must go where God sends us to go, and not just think we should go somewhere because we get an invitation. Moreover, we need to consider that there are points in our lives where we can't always go very easily. The Apostle Paul was called as an apostle for fifteen years before he set out travelling in active ministry. Does this mean he wasn't an apostle for fifteen years? No, it does not; it just means that the waiting period was a part of God's timing. The Apostle Paul and others as well also spent different periods of time in different places. We may be called to go overseas for a few weeks, and to work within the United States for several years, or we may be called to live in one country for awhile and visit others periodically...but it doesn't change our calling. Other factors, such as illness, finances, or a change in where we are being sent can also affect where we go, for how long we go, when we go, and if we go. Everything is in the timing because God is in the details.

Relationship

> **AUTHOR'S REFLECTIONS**
>
> The way guests are treated in a ministry says a lot about the church or ministry that invited them. If we are to practice what we preach, we need to make sure we are living the practices of hospitality in our own ministries.

It's a lot to expect someone who doesn't know you to minister for them, especially when it involves travelling a long distance. We don't have to be someone's best friend, but we do need more information than just an email message making various claims about a ministry and what they are doing. I explain it like this: when I am invited to speak somewhere, I go with the trust that whoever it is that has invited me won't leave me sitting at the airport in a strange place. We need to build relationships with those we speak for, no matter where in the world we are doing that.

Partnership

The Apostle Paul's ministry was funded by those who believed in what God did through him and those he supported and worked with. I know we want to pretend money has no place in ministry, but financial arrangements are a part of hospitality. Ministers should never leave an event without an offering - a best offering, not a mediocre one. If someone waives their offering because they know the host, that is different from refusing to give an offering at all, and that is an agreement reached between those two people. If we are going into an area of our own volition, without an invitation and for missions or teaching, those events are funded by our ministries, by those who believe in what we are doing, or from our own resources. In that case, the partnership is different than when we are invited.

Willingness to cover costs

In keeping with hospitality, the first-century ministries did not pay for their travel or housing when going to churches or church events. Today we should never invite someone to an event and expect they will cover their transportation and hotel accommodation. If someone knows a situation and insists on paying for themselves, that is between them and the host - but in being hospitable, a host should be willing to cover those expenses without question. If a host can't cover that expense, they should not invite others to minister. As we clarified earlier, "I don't have the money" is not an excuse. We don't ask people to pay for themselves - if they want to, that is up to them - but we never ask that of someone in the spirit of hospitality. If you don't have it by yourself, get together with some other people and bring it to pass. Everyone can bring forth what they have, and God can make it enough!

Making guests comfortable

When transcending cultures, we need to consider the standards for hospitality in our modern age. The hotel has become the international standard for travelling hospitality. If someone is transcending a culture and used to a different diet, we must consider that as well - and, once again, a hotel answers that question. Asking someone to just 'make do' with certain accommodation because you don't want to be out the money is unacceptable. It doesn't need to be a five-star resort, but it does need to be clean, bug-free, and reputable. In preaching, provide water or something to drink for the minister. Don't expect a minister to bring their own water!

God calls us to hospitality!

God calls us to hospitality! Ministers are called to receive hospitality! That is His way. Rich or poor, we offer it. We do our best for Him because we trust Him. Instead of echoing the First Church of More which seems to be prevalent everywhere, we ALL need to learn a bigger lesson about the call to give and to receive. When we are hospitable, we are blessed. Maybe we are seeing so many problems and lack of blessings all around in the church - in every country - because we have forgotten the long-lost call to hospitality. I'm voting for a hospitality revival, praise God! It starts with us - and every event we have, attend, and raising up the standards God has commanded to His people.

Apostle Marino preaching in Florence, South Carolina (January 2012)

24 THE BATTLE BELONGS TO THE LORD
(Volume 9, Number 7—July 2010)

One day I was innocently doing the work of ministry. I was minding my business, causing no harm. Then all of a sudden, the apostle I'd been under announced she was no longer covering me after she'd behaved strangely for weeks. I was told I would not be speaking at a conference because the host wanted to take money from our work as part of the event. Someone I had called several months earlier - and never returned my phone call - called me out of the blue and turned the conversation around as if I was the one who had done something to him. Mail got lost, my dog started acting up, and I experienced battle in my home. It was as if the whole host of hell decided it was time to pay me a visit.

All this came right after I decided it was time to take some positive steps forward in my ministry. I took a step forward, and the enemy sought to make me go five or six steps backward. I stepped out in faith, and in an attempt to cause massive discouragement, the enemy brought forth his best attack.

There was a time when this sudden splurge of warfare would have caused me great discouragement. This time I did not experience that discouragement. What I did experience was an intense sense of pressing in and being serious in the work of the Lord. It was a confirmation, rather than a diversion.

My personal story of warfare is not uncommon today. I'm hearing of a regular increase of people who report intense spiritual battle and warfare. In a recent week, I received no less than six different prayer requests and testimonies from people battling with spiritual forces. People who are familiar with spiritual warfare recognize an increase in tumult and struggle with the forces of darkness. People who are not so familiar with spiritual battle are more confused about the disturbing circumstances that seem to rise up and attempt to conquer areas of their lives.

> **BEHIND THE ARTICLE**
>
> Spiritual warfare remains a popular topic in most Christian circles, even today. Recognizing its relevance in the life of the believer, I wanted to teach on spiritual warfare, just from a different point of view. The result was this article.

The popular worship song, *The Battle Belongs to the Lord* could rightly be called the Christian's battle anthem. It epitomizes the strength, focus, character, and spiritual power we need to fight evil every day of our lives. We hear a lot about "spiritual warfare" as Christians, particularly in the context of the times we are living in. Living in the end times poses unique challenges to this age. These last days are filled with evil bombardments all around, just as 2 Timothy 3:2-5 said they would: *People will be lovers of themselves, lovers of money, boastful, proud, abusive, disobedient to their parents, ungrateful, unholy, without love, unforgiving, slanderous, without self-control, brutal, not lovers of the good, treacherous, rash, conceited, lovers of pleasure rather than lovers of God - having a form of godliness but denying its power.* These times are as near to us as the morning newspaper or visit to the latest internet news site. This means being a true blood-bought Christian everyday requires a special preparation as we engage in war against the forces of evil. The spiritual realm for battle is stronger, fiercer, and more vengeful than ever before. It also most importantly leans we must know spiritual warfare, the true enemies we fight, and we must know Who the battle belongs to and Who we are fighting for.

The order of battle

The War of the Sons of Light With the Sons of Darkness is an epic drama describing the great battle between light and dark, or good and evil forces. Found in the original writings of the Dead Sea Scrolls, this book describes the different orders in which the troops would assemble for battle and what purposes each group would serve to the battle. While the book is too long to post in its entirety, I encourage all of you to read it in order to understand a few essential things about spiritual battle, the purpose, and priorities we must have. Too often spiritual warfare is spoken of as a haphazard grouping of events that are simultaneously thrown into spiritual prayer. Spiritual warfare is ordered and disciplined, as is every aspect of the Christian life. Just as natural battle takes strategy and skill, so does spiritual battle. We can't attack an enemy without knowing Who we fight for, how we fight, and who that enemy is.

The War of the Sons of Light With the Sons of Darkness reminds us, *Yours is the battle, and from You is Power, and it is not ours; nor has our strength or the might of our hands done valiantly, but it is by Your strength and by the Power of Your great might; as you made known to us of old...*[1] Many Christians falter in spiritual battle due to disordered unpreparedness. They forget to Whom the battle belongs and whereby we acquire strength for the battle. Recognizing God as the central aspect to battle - and knowing His precepts for divine order - are the first steps to establishing powerful battle strategies. Living in disobedience to the Father and His precepts opens one up to spiritual defeat.

Christians also need to realize we are not to fight God's battle for our own personal ego gain, glory, or to bring something unto ourselves that is not of God. As we grow in spiritual battle, we find the fight is against the impressions of the flesh, and therefore, growing in battle means we become less impressionable to the wrong desires and more powerful in the things of God. As we submit ourselves to our heavenly Father, we learn more and more about how to become a victorious Kingdom warrior.

Who are we fighting?

Knowing the battle belongs to God is just the beginning of effective warfare. Who are we fighting? Do we merely fight against annoying people, personality conflicts, or little irritants? Ephesians 6:12 helps us to identify the true enemy: *For our struggle is not against flesh and blood, but against the rulers, against the authorities, against the powers of this dark world and against the spiritual forces of evil in the heavenly realms.* We don't merely fight people, but the evil they support, enable, channel, or cooperate with

---

KEY VERSE: EPHESIANS 6:12

For our struggle is not against flesh and blood, but against the rulers, against the authorities, against the powers of this dark world and against the spiritual forces of evil in the heavenly realms.

through their choices, words, and actions. Everything is greater than ourselves and we all represent a principle greater than ourselves. It is our choice whether those principles are of God or Satan. Whether we are fighting for light or darkness shows in our choices and behavior. That having been said, we recognize every choice we make is a form of warfare right along with prayer, worship, intercession, spiritual preparation, casting out devils and demons, and showing genuine love for God and others. Everything we do is either a mark for right or wrong. We do not act alone, nor do we make our choices alone. Even though we do all we do by free will, we agree with light or dark, and we choose to either agree with the Lord and Master of the Universe or the lord and master of this age. Which side we agree with determines where we choose to place or will and the victory we either will or will not have in our lives.

How do we prepare for battle?

If we know Who the battle is for and recognize we must choose our side, how do we then prepare for battle? God's Word gives us the answer. Ephesians 6:10-11 and 13 tell us, *Finally, be strong in the Lord and in His mighty power. Put on the full armor of God so that you can take your stand against the devil's schemes...Therefore put on the full armor of God so that when the day of evil comes, you may be able to stand your ground, and after you have done everything, to stand.* We must be strong in the Lord's strength, His power, and put on the full armor of God. The first key to preparing for battle, therefore, is making sure we leave no part of us exposed. Areas of weakness and parts of us in need of healing become grounds for Satan to target us in battle. If we make a point to put on the full armor of God, no part of us will be left exposed. Then we will be prepared for anything the enemies of God may throw at us!

    I know whenever I hear the word "armor" I immediately think of the knights of old who rode on horseback and wore complete metal suits in order to protect their bodies from primitive warfare devices. From their heads to their toes they were completely covered and protected against spears, swords, and primitive explosives. Then, in addition to these protective items worn on the body, they also carried defense items, such as swords and spears. It is no accident that the armor of God discussed in Ephesians 6 uses the same type of thorough completeness in its description of God's armor available to every Christian. We must be completely prepared and covered for our defenses and offenses in spiritual battle. It also tells us that we must put on the armor of God. In other words, we must prepare ourselves. Preparing ourselves with spiritual armor is our job. The armor of God does not just jump on us and do the work for us. We must make the effort to be prepared.

The armor for warfare

Ephesians 6:14-17 states: *Stand firm, then, with the belt of truth buckled around your waist, with the breastplate of righteousness in place, and with your feet fitted with the readiness that comes from the Gospel of peace. In addition to all this, take up the shield of faith, with which you can extinguish all the flaming arrows of the evil one. Take the helmet of salvation and the sword of the Spirit, which is the word of God.* Notice the armor of God covers us defensively. It gives us the opportunity to stand firm and ready. The backside of a soldier is not covered for spiritual battle because we address the battle head-on. There is no call and no room to turn and flee. God calls us to address spiritual battle head-on. We cannot be cowards, fearful of what lies ahead.

The belt of truth holds us up as our foundation to stand. The breastplate of righteousness covers the heart and the inwardness of life, proving righteousness is an awesome protection of the character and inwardness of man. The shoes of peace carry us in peace as a firm foundation. We can stand in truth as we are protected by righteousness. This gives us the opportunity to walk in complete peace, not fettered or worried about worldly cares. The helmet of salvation protects our minds and thoughts. As Christians, we are called to *put on the mind of Christ* (1 Corinthians 2:16). In so doing, we transform our thoughts, our understanding, and the way we look at things, and the way we reason situations to examine and focus more deeply on the spiritual things of God. The helmet of salvation protects our minds and thoughts as we think and focus. It also protects our vision so we may see, our ears may hear, and our mouths may speak correctly and come at the enemy with verbal force. We also see mention of the sword of the Spirit, which we are told is the Word of God. It is no accident Hebrews 4:12 reiterates this fact: *For the Word of God is living and active. Sharper than any double-edged sword, it penetrates even to the dividing soul and spirit, joints and marrow; it judges the thoughts and attitudes of the heart.* The shield of faith is our protective outer barrier. We hold the shield in front of us, moving it to deter the darts and sneers of the enemy and his workers. As we hold it before us, the shield of faith is a visible and defensive sign that separates us from evil. This is of the utmost importance! We can never hide our faith or we will experience an enemy attack. When we hide our faith, as many do in certain circumstances, we hide our most visible defense against evil. We should ALWAYS place our faith before us, in every situation that arises, as one of our most essential aspects to spiritual warfare.

When we put on the full armor of God, we are fully protected. Receiving God's full protection begins and ends with our choice. We must make the choice to put on God's armor and the choice to stand and fight.

We must make the conscious choice to remain standing and fighting, even when the battle is difficult or seems undesirable. What we must recognize is when we are fully armored, nothing of the enemy can come against us. We must remain aware, constantly vigilant to protect ourselves spiritually.

A special kind of prayer is needed!

> **AUTHOR'S REFLECTIONS**
>
> We talk so much about spiritual warfare and spiritual battles around us that we've forgotten how to be effective in battle. Consistency is key. Don't work so hard to figure out where the enemy lies or get so paranoid that you feel insecure. Spiritual battle should make us aware of things to push us on to greater faith, not make us afraid.

In finishing the passage from Ephesians 6, verse 18 reads: *And pray in the Spirit on all occasions with all kinds of prayers and requests. With this in mind, be alert and always keep on praying for all the saints.* Prayer is our constant communication with God, and what we must do all through battle. It provides refreshment, stamina, endurance, and spiritual sustenance. Prayer helps us to keep praising right through to the very end. Yet we are told here in Ephesians 6:18 a special kind of prayer is needed for effective warfare: prayer in the Spirit. We must pray in the Spirit, and in agreement with the Spirit of God. As we use the gift of praying in tongues and praying through other spiritual means (such as music, dance, or spoken prayer), we recognize we are always praying for whatever is in need, within ourselves and the saints of God. While it is very effective to pray in tongues for this accomplished purpose, one can pray in the Spirit no matter what language we speak. The key to prayer in the Spirit is the intent, *Not my will, but Thine be done* (Matthew 26:39, KJV) as we verbalize that will, be it in English or tongues. In battle, the key to success lies in focusing on God's will spiritually, emotionally, and physically in our lives. Through this realization, we see what to fight and the specific strategy necessary to defeat the enemy. Prayer in the Spirit is the beginning, sustainer, and every soldier who fights in the battle belonging to the Lord for this reason: it is by prayer in the Spirit that we recognize God's will and stay connected to it all throughout the struggle.

The requirements for spiritual battle remain the same

We live in a world where we like to avoid inconvenience and difficulty. We don't like being called out of our comfort zone and we especially dislike being called to do something such as active spiritual battle. Active battle calls us to discipline and set aside our own personal wants and unwillingness to go the extra mile for the greater glory of God. Society has changed in its habits of alertness and willingness. We rely on alarm systems, professional watch organizations, and others to perform the task of diligence so we don't have to sacrifice personal convenience, time, and comfort. Too many Christians have followed these modern trends. We want pastors and other church leaders to stand on the watch for spiritual matters and hold them accountable for our trials and battles. Spiritual battle does not work like this and never has. The battle of God has not changed! We are constantly called to choose sides in every action, step, and experience we take. Too many Christians side with Satan, even unknowingly, motivated by a lazy and slothful spirit. We must never forget Christians are called to be an excellent people, modeling the excellence of God in all we do. We are not called to be a mediocre group that barely gets by and barely makes any lasting imprint on the world we're in. It is not uncommon to encounter such compromised Christians who want nothing more than to be unbothered and ignore the choices God asks us to make. All they wind up doing is leaving themselves open to spiritual invasion from the evil one, as they fail to protect themselves with the armor of God. We only bring about the changes we desire in our spiritual lives and this world as a whole if we make conscious commitment to fight on the Lord's side. We can either make our choices accordingly and benefit from all God has for us as soldiers on His side of the war, or we can leave ourselves open to the point where each choice is a crisis and we turn on God.

    The victory is won, battle by battle, in our lives. The key is persistence and never giving up. While the requirements for spiritual battle haven't changed, the benefits of fighting the battle have not changed, either. We are still privy to the blessings, prosperity, and wonders of life wrought in the victory of defeating the devil in spiritual battle. Let's go toward that victory that is ours in Christ! In the words of the great old hymn, Onward, Christian Soldiers!

---

[1]*The War With The Sons Of Light With The Sons Of Darkness* as found in *The Other Bible*, edited by Willis Barnstone. San Francisco, California: Harper Collins San Francisco, 1984.

Apostle Marino during a television/internet interview in Beerta, the Netherlands (March 2013)

25 IT'S THE END OF THE WORLD AS WE KNOW IT
(Volume 12, Number 13 – Fourth Quarter 2014)

In 1987, the rock band R.E.M. sang us a song about the various "streams of consciousness" that flash before our eyes daily, titled: *End Of The World As We Know It (And I Feel Fine)*. Front man Michael Stipes stated in 1992 that the song's inspiration came from "channel flipping" and recounting the various things that enter into our thoughts within a daily span. Verse 2 of the song contains the following lyrics: "*Six o'clock, TV hour, don't get caught in foreign tower/Slash and burn, return, listen to yourself churn Lock him in uniform, book burning, bloodletting/Every motive escalate, automotive incinerate/Light a candle, light a motive, step down, step down/Watch your heel crush, crush, uh-oh/This means no fear, cavalier, renegade and steering clear/A tournament, a tournament, a tournament of lies/Offer me solutions, offer me alternatives, and I decline.*"

Even though the song is almost thirty years old, R.E.M. was on to something when they sang about these different "streams of consciousness" and the way in which they impact how we view the world around us. If we watch the news today, it seems like we are surrounded by a never-ending stream of bad news: war, poverty, drugs, anger, hostility, intolerance, politics, economic disaster, and yes, hypocrisy on the part of every religion under the sun. But does all this mean that the world is "ending?" What does it all mean in the scope of the prophetic and of Bible prophecy? If things are coming to a "close," of sorts, how should we face it - and how should we prepare?

A continual phenomenon

What do the years 389, 793, 1260, 1528, 1705, 1792, 1806, 1814, 1836, 1843, 1874, 1914, 1918, 1920, 1954, 1969, 1977, 1982, 1988, 1994, 1999, 2000, 2011 and 2012 all have in common? They were all years in which someone out there predicted the "end of the world" would come. Whether coming to such a conclusion by observing world events or via a claim of private revelation (a vision, discovery or study, or a dream), people surrounding these years in history were absolutely convinced that the world was going to end as a result of what they perceived. Most people who advocated the "end" in these years wrote books or literature, engaged in preaching or public speaking, and exposed their viewpoints in some specific way as part of their proclamation about the end. While they might have been sincere people who truly believed something had been revealed to them, history clearly doesn't support whatever it is they feel they heard or saw. These years and their various dates, predictions or findings behind them, and the individuals who made such predictions have almost entirely passed away.

> **BEHIND THE ARTICLE**
>
> One thing I love about this anthology is seeing the different ways in which I have evolved in my understanding as a minister and as a preacher. This article, which was featured in our last edition of 2014, displays just that. While I have spoken on the end times frequently throughout the history of *Power For Today* Magazine, this article sums up best the most balanced, practical way to approach such teaching when we encounter it in the world.

It would appear that many people today follow the same suit as their predecessors. They may be genuinely sincere, earnest in their studies and findings, truly believing they have been sent with a message for our day and age. While the specific targets they point to as signs of accuracy may be different, the underlying message is always the same - "THE END IS NEAR!" The verses used are always almost the same, despite the fact it is many years later and the events involve different people and technology. Knowing this fact of history, what should it tell us about analyzing "signs of the times?" Also, how can we know the "day and hour" in which we live? Who can we trust in these matters?

The final hour

In 1 John 2:18, the Apostle John writes the following words: *Little children, it is the last hour. Just as you have heard that the antichrist is coming, so now many antichrists have appeared. This is how we know it is the last hour.* (CEB) It's obvious from reading the Word that Christians in the New Testament believed Jesus would return in their lifetimes. They believed that all the signs around them pointed to His immediate return. I am sure if you interviewed a first-century Christian about when Jesus was to return, they would have all agreed He would have long returned by now. Even though this might sound like many Christians who have been alive throughout history, there is one major difference between first-century believers and believers today, and that is the result of such a belief. First-century Christians believed the impending return of Christ needed to alert the church to attend to its own duties: proclaim the Kingdom of heaven is at hand and do the work of the Kingdom. It wasn't to run wild, sell a lot of books, create general hysteria or a mass following of people. Knowing and recognizing the times was not for the purpose of sensationalism but was for the purpose of building up solidarity and knowing we only have a limited amount of time to proclaim the Kingdom.

That certainly sounds like a stark contrast in comparison with what we see today, isn't it? It seems like the "end times" is a big ploy to sell books, audio CD series, and spark a renewed frenzy in a ministry setting that has grown stale. It was also not to push a political agenda (quite the opposite, in fact), and also not to endorse an escapist, "let's get out of this world" kind of attitude. The reason for alerting the church to the "final hour" isn't for any of the reasons so many attempt to use it for today. The church of the first century needed constant reminders to stay focused on its task, as it was constantly distracted by everything around it. Thus, today, we need the same reminder for the final hour, not for a new reason, but for the same exact one.

KEY VERSE: 1 JOHN 2:18

Little children, it is the last hour. Just as you have heard that the antichrist is coming, so now many antichrists have appeared. This is how we know it is the last hour. (CEB)

Maintaining the status quo

One constant struggle we see in the Bible: only a select few in history were willing to be different enough to make an impact on the world around them. There's a reason we hear about the same people over and over again in Bible teaching and study: because there were only a few individuals throughout the course of history who were truly noteworthy enough to make the Biblical record. The same is true today: people may sound good, look good, walk the walk, and talk the talk on the surface, but when it comes to truly living a life that merits a Kingdom impact, we don't see much of that. People are quick to jump on a current bandwagon and post spiritual-looking pictures all over Facebook, but the Bible itself tells us most people aren't living the way they should. Matthew 24:36-39 confirms this fact: *But of that day and hour knoweth no man, no, not the angels of heaven, but my Father only. But as the days of Noah were, so shall also the coming of the Son of man be. For as in the days that were before the flood they were eating and drinking, marrying and giving in marriage, until the day that Noe entered into the ark, And knew not until the flood came, and took them all away; so shall also the coming of the Son of man be."* (KJV) The people of Noah's time went on their merry way, doing the same things they always did, right up until the time it was too late. In this age, therefore, before Jesus returns, people will follow in a like-minded course. They will do the things they want to do, following the status quo that is their life. People will continue to get married, have families, go to work, and engage in whatever actions they desire. Powers, controlling interests, and paradigms will shift multiple times, as life continues like it has...since time began. No matter who is in charge or what ruling power seems to be dominant, the Bible makes it clear that time will go on, until it is too late.

This means that people who sound right - the people who cry about the end times the loudest - are included in those who are just "going along," like everyone else. I believe many people feel the "end is at hand" today because more traditional powers that be are quickly fading away and being replaced by new trends. Whether these trends are good or not is not the point; the point is that people do not like change.

I think at the root of much modern end-time teaching is a fear-based reaction toward loss of control. As the world shifts and changes, new laws, regulations, and values start to come into place. People don't want to lose the comforts they have forever learned to associate with life. As a result, the battle rages for control and people want, more and more, to simply escape from the discomforts they experience as a result of change.

Do we properly understand the "time of the end?"

Many years ago I interviewed a woman as part of a religion interview about her general doctrinal beliefs. When I asked her if she believed we were in the end times/latter days, her response to me was, "Sure looks like it, but it's looked like it before, and people were wrong. I guess if it is, we'll find out, and if it's not, we'll still be here." Her words resonated with me, and I believe they contain wisdom for us today, almost fifteen years later. It's fine, even Biblical, for us to recognize the times in which we live. It is not Biblical to spend our lives running around like Henny Penny, promising the world the "sky is falling."

What does it mean to be in the "end times?" The prophecies can seem vague and confusing, the changing times can cause us to think we are further along in the process than we are, and it can I think, as believers, it is important we understand just what that means so we can live our lives out properly in these days. Despite the way the prophecies are written, there are a couple of things we can - and should - keep in mind when assessing these days.

- **Prophecy can't be "plugged" into a headline** - Attempting to take specific Bible verses and "plug" them into current events headlines has become popular over the past fifty years. This is a total distortion of how prophecy works. Prophetic words don't fit neatly into a headline. We can't read a Bible verse and immediately associate it with a current event. What the Bible encourages us to do is know the prophecy and recognize the times. That means we interpret prophecy according to many different things it has revealed, rather than trying to break it apart and assign it to one thing. Prophecy doesn't state there will be one natural disaster, but a series of different natural events, both natural and supernatural, at that. Certain spiritual and political events come along with the times. Other things are enclosed in prophetic precepts, veiled in symbology we don't readily understand and often have questions about. Take prophecy one step at a time and realize prophecy is a revelation, not a headline to sell newspapers or magazines.

- **Avoid chasing after every trend of end times doctrine** - One of Jesus' most often ignored commands (and yes, it was a command) is Mark 13:5-6: *"See to it that no one misleads you. Many will come in My name, saying, 'I am He!' and will mislead many."* (NASB) It's no accident that Jesus says this prior to discussing the various signs to come and the different things that will be a part of the end times. Too many of us (me included) have been guilty of following various end time trends, following different teachers or individuals who told us this, that, and something else, all of which was questionable, false, or some combination of the two. False prophets are a practical, visible sign of the last days. While it's easy to point out who you think is wrong with a leader by a short, simple assessment of their overall teachings, consider this: very well-known and well-respected historical figures, including Jonathan Edwards and John Wesley, all falsely predicted the Second Coming within their lifetimes. As people, we must carefully examine teachings and beware swallowing anyone's teaching whole without giving it consideration and weighing it in the light of Biblical revelation and also common sense.

- **Use Biblical prophecy about the last days to examine yourself and what you involve yourself with** - When Jesus is returning is not our business. It has nothing to do with us. The day and the hour it's happening are not our business. Who the antichrist, beast of revelation, and whore of Babylon are aren't, believe it or not, that relevant to understanding the prophecies. If who they were was to be that specified, it would be laid out in the Scriptures in black and white. God has had His people prophecy about these things so we will look at ourselves and what we choose to follow, not so we'll point fingers at everyone else to make sure others think they are wrong about what they teach. Biblical prophecy about the antichrist, the beast of revelation, and the whore of Babylon has been translated differently throughout history, and rightly so. The way these prophecies are worded, they can apply to multiple things. We are warned about these things to be on our guard and to ensure we don't go chasing after every wind of false doctrine, not to offend other people.

- **Prophecy is not a timeline** - The ancients viewed prophecy as circular or cyclical, not linear. They did not think of prophetic events as happening in a nice, neat order, but as things that came around every so often. The whole concept of the "end times" is actually not the end of a line of events, as is often portrayed today. The term "end times" is actually a play on both Greek and Hebrew terms that relate to the "end of the age" or "end of the current system." It represents a paradigm shift, humanity passing from one cycle, or era of governance, to another. In other words, the end times signifies the passing of the world from being under the control, dominion, and influence of Satan to being under the influence of Jesus. This is the ultimate restoration of all things spoken about by the Apostle

Peter in the book of Acts: the world, and the people therein, shall be finally in a restored and perfected state, where they are no longer affected by sin. The end times represent the transition between these worlds and powers. The result is conflict, all around us: in our governments, in our international relations, in our natural elements and natural weather patterns, in our relationships with one another, within the dynamics and teachings of the church, and in the general function of day-to-day living. The world needs to be set aright, but the way in which it happens won't follow a nice, neat timeline. It may seem like we are in one place prophetically at one time, and in a totally different place at another. Some events happen simultaneously, others rise and fall, like the workings of a plot line in a story. Start thinking of prophecy as the cycle of the ages, and the end times as a part of that prophetic cycle, rather than trying to fit everything into a modern, chronological timeline.

- **Do not be afraid** - Mark 13:33-37 says, *Take heed, keep on the alert; for you do not know when the appointed time will come. It is like a man away on a journey, who upon leaving his house and putting his slaves in charge, assigning to each one his task, also commanded the doorkeeper to stay on the alert. Therefore, be on the alert—for you do not know when the master of the house is coming, whether in the evening, at midnight, or when the rooster crows, or in the morning— in case he should come suddenly and find you asleep. What I say to you I say to all, 'Be on the alert!* (NASB) There is a marked difference between being aware and on alert, knowing the things which are going on around you versus being afraid of everything that is going on around you. We are not warned about the end times so that we can be people who are afraid of everything, from new ideas to education to the world at large. It is not God's will that we buy into fear tactics that were solely created so we'll support the agenda of a public or notable figure who wants to maintain a sense of control. The things that go on in this world are things that do just that - go on. None of them are new. On the contrary, all of them have been done for generations and generations; the only difference is that in times past, we never heard about many of them. We have no reason to be afraid, because nothing is new and will forever have the same results. What we are called to do is stand - not flee.

- **Aim for accuracy** - The New Testament letters were written by Christians, to other Christians, to talk about other Christians. There is no such thing as a "Muslim antichrist." If the antichrist comes forth from the church, there is no way the antichrist represents a secular political power. These may seem like little details, but the truth is that prophecy is in the details. Changing who the antichrist is every couple of years isn't a sign of accurate prophecy, it's the sign of inaccurate interpretation. No matter how "perfect" it may seem to fit with those plugged-in headlines, reject teaching that doesn't fit nor follow the heart of true prophetic accuracy.

What end times prophecy teaches us about ourselves

> **AUTHOR'S REFLECTIONS**
>
> Writing about the end times is never easy, especially when the perspective presented is often radically different from what has come to be standard as pertains to such teaching. It's important, however, for all of us to stop using last days doctrine to point fingers at other people, to offend others, to stand out as rude or unseemly to others, or to run and escape from the work that God has us to do. Last days or not, the work of the Christian remains the same right up until the time when Jesus comes back.

Prophecy is, before all other things, a mirror for us to look at ourselves in. When it comes to end times prophecy, this "mirror" we are called to examine ourselves in is no different. We are called to look at what we believe, who we follow, and what kind of teaching we entertain. In Jude 1:8-13, we learn: *Yet, in a similar way, the people who slipped in among you are dreamers. They contaminate their bodies with sin, reject the Lord's authority, and insult his glory. When the archangel Michael argued with the devil, they were arguing over the body of Moses. But Michael didn't dare to hand down a judgment against the devil. Instead, Michael said, "May the Lord reprimand you!" Whatever these people don't understand, they insult. Like animals, which are creatures of instinct, they use whatever they know to destroy themselves. How horrible it will be for them! They have followed the path of Cain. They have rushed into Balaam's error to make a profit. They have rebelled like Korah and destroyed themselves. These people are a disgrace at the special meals you share with other believers. They eat with you and don't feel ashamed. They are shepherds who care only for themselves. They are dry clouds blown around by the winds. They are withered, uprooted trees without any fruit. As a result, they have died twice. Their shame is like the foam on the wild waves of the sea. They are wandering stars for whom gloomy darkness is kept forever."* (GW) Not one of these verses tells us to run out and wear a sign that says, "THE END IS NEAR." It does caution us to realize that even within the midst of our closest fellowships, connections, and yes, those that may appear to think the most like us - we are going to see and face people who are not truly with us. We need to take inventory of who is around us, what we believe, who we fellowship with, and be on our guard against being led astray.

No matter what you may believe about the doctrine of the end times (and we all know there are a wide array of beliefs on the subject), the bottom line of it all is to dedicate oneself even more than ever before to the work of the Gospel. It's time to stop waiting for someone else to do the work of the Kingdom and rise up to do what God has called you to do, because we are aware that time as we understand it today is quickly running out. God calls each and every one of His believers to be good stewards with our resources, and nothing should cause us to be as aware as the need for that as the day and hour in which we are living. The end times should make us want to live our faith and live it right. Love is not just a four-letter word; it is something we are called to live as Kingdom people, in an era where people need love and the presence of God more than they ever have before. We must make the most of the time we have left, so we can hear the words, *Good job! You're a good and faithful servant! You proved that you could be trusted with a small amount. I will put you in charge of a large amount. Come and share your master's happiness* (Matthew 25:21, GW) when it is all said and done.

---

[1]*R.E.M. Lyrics: End Of The World As We Know It (And I Feel Fine)* as found at http://www.azlyrics.com/lyrics/rem/itstheendoftheworldasweknowitandifeelfine.html. Accessed November 10, 2014.

Apostle Marino preaching in Greenville, North Carolina (October 2010)

ABOUT THE AUTHOR
Dr. Lee Ann B. Marino, Ph.D., D.Min., D.D.

Dr. Lee Ann B. Marino, Ph.D., D.Min., D.D. (she/her) is "everyone's favorite theologian" leading Gen X, Millennials, and Gen Z with expertise in leadership training, queer and feminist theology, general religion, and apostolic theology. She has served in ministry since 1998 and was ordained as a pastor in 2002 and an apostle in 2010. She founded what is now Sanctuary Apostolic Fellowship Empowerment (SAFE) Ministries in 2004. Under her ministry heading Dr. Marino is founder and Overseer of Sanctuary International Fellowship Tabernacle (SIFT) (the original home of National Coming Out Sunday) and The Sanctuary Network, and Chancellor of Apostolic Covenant Theological Seminary (ACTS).

Affectionately nicknamed "the Spitfire," Dr. Marino has spent over two decades as an "apostle, preacher, and teacher" (2 Timothy 1:11), exercising her personal mandate to become "all things to all people" (1 Corinthians 9:22). Her embrace of spiritual issues (both technical and intimate) has found its home among both seekers and believers, those who desire spiritual answers to today's issues.

Dr. Marino has preached throughout the United States, Puerto Rico, and Europe in hundreds of religious services and experiences throughout the years. A history maker in her own right, she has spent over two decades in advocacy, education, and work for and within minority spiritual communities (including African American, Hispanic, and LGBTQ+). She has also served as the first woman on all-male synods, councils, and panels, as well as the first preacher or speaker welcomed of a different race, sexual orientation, or identity among diverse communities. Today, Dr. Marino's work extends to over 150 countries as she hosts the popular *Kingdom Now* podcast, which is in the top 20 percentile of all podcasts worldwide. She is also the author of over 35 books and the popular Patheos column, *Leadership on Fire*. To date, she has had five bestselling titles within their subject matter: *Understanding Demonology, Spiritual Warfare, Healing, and Deliverance: A Manual for the Christian Minister;*

Ministry School Boot Camp: Training for Helps Ministries, Appointments, and Beyond; *Discovering Intimacy: A Journey Through the Song of Solomon*; *Fruit of the Vine: Study and Commentary on the Fruit of the Spirit*; and *Ministering to LGBTQ+ (and Those Who Love Them): A Primer for Queer Theology* (and its accompanying workbook).

As a public icon and social media influencer, Dr. Marino advocates healthy body image (curvy/full-figured), representation as a demisexual/aromantic, and albinism awareness as a model. Known to those she works with, she is a spiritual mom, teacher, leader, professor, confidant, and friend. She continues to transform, receiving new teaching, revelation, and insight in this thing we call "ministry." Through years of spiritual growth and maturity, Dr. Marino stands as herself, here to present what God has given to her for any who have an ear to hear.

For more information, visit her website at kingdompowernow.org.